Preventing Child Sexual Abuse

Preventing Child Sexual Abuse

A Curriculum for Children
Ages Five Through Eight

Kathryn Goering Reid

United Church Press
Cleveland, Ohio

United Church Press, Cleveland, Ohio 44115

©1994 by Kathryn Goering Reid

Illustrators: Betty Hendrick and Betsy James

Printed in the United States of America on acid-free paper

99 98 97 96 95 94   5 4 3 2 1

Library of Congress Cataloging-in-Publication Data

Reid, Kathryn Goering.
Preventing child sexual abuse : a curriculum for children
ages five through eight / Kathryn Goering Reid.
p. cm.
Includes bibliographical references and index.
ISBN 0-8298-1016-1
1. Child sexual abuse—Prevention—Study and teaching
(Elementary)—United States.
2. Child sexual abuse—Religious aspects—Christianity.
3. Christian education of children—United States—Curricula.
I. Title.
HQ72.U53R448   1994   94-3395
261.8'32—dc20   CIP

For my dad, Ozzie Goering,
whose love and care of children inspired me
to become a teacher and a pastor

Contents

Foreword

"Your children are not your children; they are the sons and daughters of life longing for itself." These words, sung by Sweet Honey in the Rock, are an important reminder to all parents that children do not *belong* to anyone; they are no one's property. While to some it may seem unnecessary to state the obvious nowadays, it is necessary nonetheless. In our society, we still live with the residue of a patriarchal culture that regarded children (and women) as men's property. The painful consequences of this heritage is the attitude that children belong to adults, that they are expendable, and that adults have sexual access to them.

Children are by definition vulnerable human beings. They are physically small; they lack physical strength and intellectual maturity as well as information; they are dependent on adults for the necessities of survival. Children trust the adults around them until they learn not to. These realities about children remain constant from generation to generation. Because of these vulnerabilities, children are easy targets for exploitation and victimization. The tragedy is that there are adults who readily take advantage of children and sexually abuse them.

There are two ways that we as responsible, caring adults can work to prevent our children from being victimized. The first is through primary prevention. We must use the criminal justice and mental health systems to intervene when necessary. We can also use the resources of the church to ensure that sexual offenders not have access to children in our church programs. But try as we may, this primary intervention will stop only a small percentage of sexual abusers.

Secondary prevention involves preparing our children to deal with a potential encounter with a sexual offender. In other words, by giving children information about the problem of child molestation and about their options, we forewarn and forearm them. By our love and support of them, we build their self-esteem. By teaching them that their bodies belong to them and that they get to choose how and when other people touch them, we encourage their self-determination.

There are some who long nostalgically for the old days when we left doors unlocked and children played safely in their neighborhoods. But we now know that in the old days children were still not safe: children were being abused then as well, and most often in their own homes by people they knew very well.

There are days when I am overwhelmed by sadness that the world is such a place that we must teach our children about this evil that might touch their lives. But better that they have knowledge they never need than that they not have knowledge that could protect them from harm.

Child sexual abuse prevention is basic safety and survival information for children. We must take the same care to teach them what to do if someone older approaches them sexually that we do in teaching them how to use matches safely and how to cross the street without being hit by a car. And whose job is this? Everyone's!

"It takes a village to raise a child." This wisdom reminds us that we all have a role to play in teaching and supporting our children. It is critical that children get information about child sexual abuse from the school, the home, and the church. Our messages should be consistent. But our particular responsibility in the church is to provide not only safety information but also a theological foundation upon which the practical information can rest. In addition, we must provide sex education to accompany abuse prevention education. We have the not-so-easy task of teaching children to celebrate the good gift of sexuality AND to seek help from us when someone tries to misuse that gift in ways that can harm them. The church finds itself in a unique and pivotal position to provide both quality sex education and sex abuse prevention training for children and young people.

Finally, it is our responsibility as church leaders to do all we can to ensure that our congregations, camps, youth events, etc., are safe places for children and young people. This demands that we carefully screen both volunteer and paid leadership and be willing to say no when the occasion requires. Ministry with children and young people is a privilege, not a right.

"Let the children come to me and do not forbid them for to these belongs the realm of God" is our Gospel call to provide for our children, to protect them in their vulnerability, to empower them in their growing, and to be a sanctuary for them in a scary world.

Pray for the courage and strength to fulfill this calling.

Rev. Marie M. Fortune

Preface

The Center for the Prevention of Sexual and Domestic Violence was founded in 1977 by an ordained minister. Its mission is to mobilize the resources of religious communities to address the widespread problems of sexual and domestic violence. To this end, the Center provides educational and training resources to denominations, local congregations, and individuals concerned about preventing abuse and violence.

One particular area of abuse prevention in which the Center has done considerable work is that of child sexual abuse. In 1984, *Sexual Abuse Prevention: A Study for Teenagers*, by Rev. Marie M. Fortune, was produced by the Center and published by United Church Press. In 1989 the Center developed *Preventing Child Sexual Abuse: Ages 9–12*, written by Kathryn Goering Reid and Rev. Marie M. Fortune in cooperation with various religious educators; it also was published by United Church Press.

This curriculum, *Preventing Child Sexual Abuse: Ages 5–8*, takes the message of abuse prevention to a younger audience. Although some may question the wisdom of raising these issues with children of this age, we believe we must. Children are vulnerable to abuse from infancy onward. Therefore, we must begin early with abuse prevention.

Some parents and other adults may raise concerns about introducing children to sexual abuse and to the concept of evil. But we must realize that children are already being introduced to evil through watching TV or talking with friends or in their own experiences. Curricula such as this one can help them begin to deal with these difficult issues within a theological and biblical context. The fact of hearing about sexual abuse in Sunday school or vacation Bible school is a powerful message to them that the church cares about this all-too-common fact of life and is there to help them deal with it.

As with our other materials, our concern is that children receive information about sexual abuse in the context of religious instruction. Many public schools now offer prevention material to children; but our concern is that in addition to the facts about sexual abuse and how to respond to it, our children receive a theological and biblical foundation for their understanding.

In addition to our curricula, the Center offers a series of videos entitled *Keeping the Faith.* These videos address religious communities and ways in which they can both prevent abuse and respond to it when it happens. Two of the four videos address child abuse. *Hear Their Cries: Religious Responses to Child Abuse* is a documentary on the role of clergy and lay leaders in responding to child abuse, and includes interviews with Jewish and Christian clergy and secular professionals, stories of adult survivors of physical and sexual abuse, a dramatic vignette demonstrating appropriate response to a victim's disclosure, and a discussion of theological issues such as forgiveness and confidentiality. *Bless the Children: Preventing Sexual Abuse* is a case study of one congregation's efforts to introduce a curriculum for child sexual abuse prevention in their Sunday school program. It stresses the role of religious institutions in preventing abuse, addresses issues of parental resistance, models appropriate responses to victims, and highlights cultural diversity issues.

The Center for the Prevention of Sexual and Domestic Violence believes that the widespread suffering experienced by victims of sexual and domestic violence represents a profound violation of persons created in God's image. The church's traditional silence has enabled it to live with the illusion that "these things don't happen to good Christian children." But they do. And our denial only means that our children suffer and grow up to be victimized again or to victimize others. These experiences of personal violence and abuse cry out for justice and for a compassionate response from the community of faith. This curriculum is one more contribution to our common ministry of justice-making and healing.

Acknowledgments

This project would have been impossible without the support, care, and vision of the women at the Center for the Prevention of Sexual and Domestic Violence in Seattle, Washington: Marie Fortune, executive director; Rebecca Voelkel, program associate; and Sandra Barone, program associate. Their enthusiasm inspired this project.

The manuscript was reviewed by the following wonderful people: L. Cecile Adams, associate council director, Detroit Conference, United Methodist Church; Dr. Gloria Durka, Fordham University, Bronx, New York; Sharon Ferrell, executive director, Child Abuse Prevention Resources, Tacoma, Washington; Dr. Ruth Harms, child abuse prevention supervisor, State Office of Superintendent of Public Instruction, State of Washington; Shirley Kirkwood; Marilyn J. Littlejohn, M.Div., MPA, Tacoma Pierce County, Commission on Children, Youth, and Their Families; Peter Shafer, pastor for Child and Parent Ministries, New Hope Church, Rochester, New York.

Special thanks to Nona May, our education consultant, who made suggestions and reviewed the materials.

Finally, without the support of my husband, Steve, and my children, Jesse, Mary, Jacob, and Derek, none of this would be finished. All of them helped by doing extra chores and giving me lots of hugs and love.

Introduction

The Problem

In recent years, our society has begun to understand the pervasiveness of child sexual abuse. It is estimated that one female child out of every three will be sexually abused before she is eighteen years old.[1] In addition, one male child out of seven will be sexually abused as well.[2] Child sexual abuse is not confined to any racial, ethnic, or socioeconomic class. Children across the world experience the nightmare of abuse.

Only now are we beginning to research the effects of abuse on children. We already know that children who are abused may grow up to abuse others. Some estimate that 75 percent of all adolescents involved in prostitution, both female and male, are survivors of prior sexual violence: rape, incestuous abuse, or molestation.[3] Over 50 percent of juvenile sex offenders are sexually or physically abused as children.[4] The abuse experienced by children, especially young children, appears to explode into countless emotional problems that affect everyone in our society.

As our awareness of the effects of child sexual abuse grows, frustrated parents and educators look for ways to prevent the abuse from happening. In order to teach prevention techniques, we are forced to examine our social, cultural, and religious attitudes about sex roles, family life, sexuality, and violence. The continuing patterns of abuse can be broken with the use of preventive education and with appropriate counseling interventions with children who have already been victimized.

The Response: Religious Education That Teaches Prevention

Education is an important aspect of effectively preventing the sexual abuse of children. Education accomplishes the following:
- It breaks through the individual and societal silence and denial that have long supported/tolerated sexual abuse of children.
- It increases access to community resources for treatment and intervention by young people.
- It decreases the level of public acceptance of sexual abuse.
- It increases the degree of understanding and awareness by children of the issues related to sexual violence.[5]

Prevention education focuses on the dissemination of factual information about child sexual abuse and the development of skills to enable a child to avoid or to resist an approach by an offender. A necessary ingredient for education is information about what to do and whom to contact for help if assaulted. Beyond these obvious goals, prevention education within a religious context offers the church an opportunity to teach children about God's care for children, about justice and forgiveness, and about the church's care for survivors.

Even though many public school are introducing prevention curricula, it is essential that the church be involved in the prevention of sexual abuse. Children who have been taught child abuse prevention in church settings report that having this information in this setting allows them to discuss values, the church's teachings, and scripture as it relates to this topic. Teaching prevention also allows the church to offer children images of hope, comfort, and healing that will be very useful to them in the future no matter what their experience.

In addition, it is important that the church no longer allow its institutions or scripture to be used to promote violence. Misinterpreted scripture or sermons are frequently used by offenders to justify sexual violence. Therefore, every avenue of communication must be used to spread the gospel message of God's love and care for children.

Purpose of This Course

Young people between the ages of five and eight are an important audience for abuse prevention education for several reasons:

- Sexual abuse begins often in early childhood.
- Children between the ages of five and eight already may have been abused sexually by a family member or by a friend or acquaintance. If so, they need information and permission to seek help in order to break out of their isolation and private pain.

This course is intended to provide information about sexual abuse and its prevention to children between the ages of five and eight in the context of a religious education program. Too many children either have been victims of sexual abuse themselves or have friends who have experienced abuse.

The purpose of this curriculum is to provide sexual abuse prevention materials to be used specifically as part of a religious education program. The ten sessions can be fit into a typical Sunday morning church school program. However, the materials could also be used as curriculum for a special event, such as summer vacation Bible school, after-school programs, or camping programs. The material is written for a limited age group and is developmentally appropriate for these ages. The oral and written activities include activities for all ages in this group.

The curriculum draws on excellent secular materials and, at the same time, uses biblical materials as resources. This material also confronts misinterpretations of biblical materials that have been used to support abusive relationships. Even if a child has had abuse prevention in school, important religious and theological ideas should be discussed and examined. Through the church's education program, prevention techniques can be taught in an environment of God's caring and supportive community.

Theology and Sexual Abuse Prevention

Many texts in the Bible speak to modern-day readers about God's support and care for survivors. Yet survivors of abuse themselves often raise challenges as they question our concepts of an all-powerful God, authority, and forgiveness. It is only natural that survivors of violence look for answers to these basic religious questions that all humankind struggles to answer: Why does God allow suffering? Why did this happen to me?

In addition to questions about basic theological concepts, the stories from women and men who have survived abuse often tell us of the comforting power of God. Images of God as comforter and healer helped them survive and helped them heal.

You shall not abuse any widow or orphan. If you do abuse them, when they cry out to me, I will surely hear their cry. [Exodus 22:22–23]

Hebrew Scripture reminds us that God does hear the cries of those who suffer. However, all too often the church has not been prepared to help survivors of sexual violence. Our teachings are misinterpreted by offenders; our sermons too often leave the survivor feeling as though God is punishing him or her for past sins and offenses. Even when we want to help, we lack the skills to effectively help survivors of violence.

Our religious education programs, established to teach our children our Christian values, reflect our lack of attention to issues of sexual violence. Nothing is more moving than to look at a church filled with small, happy children and remember the overpowering statistics about sexual violence in this country. One out of three girls and one of seven boys will experience the nightmare of sexual violence. How many children in our church school classes already have experienced abuse? How many of their friends have experienced abuse?

This curriculum is written specifically as a response from the Christian community to the pervasive sexual violence that our children experience. Even though schools teach sexual abuse prevention, our task in religious education programs is to teach our children more than factual information about abuse. Our task is to teach them that God loves each child, that God is a comforter to those who suffer, that the church is God's community of people who care for others, and that each of us, male and female, is created in God's image.

That is why Bible study, worship, and prayer are included in each and every session. This is not just redone secular material. Rather, our theology stands at the core of this curriculum. This curriculum reflects our basic belief that we are all created in God's image, that children are special to God, and that God seeks justice for the survivor and repentance for the offender.

This curriculum is also rooted in the theological concept that all people are created in God's image. It is therefore essential that our theology be inclusive of all people, both male and female. Scriptures cited are from the New Revised Standard Version.

Planning for This Course

The curriculum unit is organized into ten sessions and is designed for teaching within a compact series of meetings (such as vacation Bible school) or in consecutive weekly meetings (such as Sunday morning church school).

Each session is divided into three sections:

Getting Started
Developing the Session
Concluding the Session

In addition to teaching objectives and a variety of activities, the lessons contain theological concepts, scriptures, prayers, songs, and other forms of worship experiences for young children. The lessons are designed to involve children, so that they may learn through participation in small-group activities, questions, and general discussions.

Session Topics

Session 1:   God Cares About Children
Session 2:   God Created Me!
Session 3:   Why Bad Things Happen to People
Session 4:   God Wants Me to Be Safe
Session 5:   God's Gift of Feelings
Session 6:   Good Touch/Bad Touch/Confusing Touch
Session 7:   God Gives Us Courage
Session 8:   No More Secrets
Session 9:   Justice and Forgiveness: Responding to Harm
Session 10: Wrapping Up with a Positive Self-Image

Leadership: Tips and Guidelines

1. Special Training in Abuse Prevention

Even when a teacher has a great deal of experience teaching in a church school program, it is highly recommended that the individual have some special training with abuse prevention techniques. Training can be obtained at workshops on child sexual abuse, from local training groups for public school teachers such as Child Abuse Prevention (CAP), or from similar organizations.

Two videotapes are particularly helpful for teachers, parents, and ministers involved with this course. *Hear Their Cries* gives basic information about child sexual abuse and the church's response. The study guide contains supportive information and discussion questions that are intended to be the basis for training sessions. *Bless the Children* is a videotape on teaching child sexual abuse to children in the church. Both tapes would be helpful preparation for all adults. These videotapes are available from the Center for the Prevention of Sexual and Domestic Violence, 1914 North 34th Street, Suite 105, Seattle, Washington 98103.

If training is not available, it is important that the teachers at least be familiar with the topic of sexual abuse (see "Resources" at the back of the book).

2. Responding to Disclosures of Child Abuse

Given the present scope of child sexual abuse in our society, it is probable that at least one child in a class will either have experienced some kind of abuse or know of someone who has. Therefore, it is essential that each leader know what to do and how to respond if a child discloses the abuse he or she has suffered; see Appendix C, "How to Help Child Victims."

3. Personal Attitudes About Sexuality

Naturally, it is important that the teachers are themselves comfortable with discussing such topics as body parts, sexual violence, incest, assault, and sexual intercourse. It is essential that the children feel comfortable discussing these issues with the teacher. A teacher who knows the group members well has an advantage.

4. Team Teaching Method

It is recommended that two people teach the curriculum. A male-female team, working together, allows flexibility in dividing into smaller groups. There may be big differences in the maturity, sophistication, and experience of the children. Depending on the maturity, a group may need to be divided along gender lines. For the various activities, the male or female leader can take different roles or lead different small groups.

5. Cultural Diversity

Although sexual abuse takes place in almost all cultures, cultural factors can influence teaching sexual abuse prevention. For example, in many cultures, there is a reticence to discuss sex. Although this curriculum has been written for children in a broad spectrum of cultures, it is impossible to take into account all cultural influences in one sexual abuse curriculum. The leader must recognize the various cultures represented in the group of children and be prepared to recognize those that challenge or enhance teaching of sexual abuse prevention.

6. Storytelling in the Classroom

The central piece in each session is the biblical story. Many teachers are accustomed to telling the story in a traditional style that utilizes verbal expressiveness, hand gestures, and eye contact as the basic way to convey meaning. This kind of storytelling requires learning the details in the story so that it comes alive for the children. Many teachers find that props such as puppets, flannel graphs, and biblical pictures are wonderful additions to help the story process.

In recent years, other styles of storytelling have become very popular. In particular, Jerome W. Berryman[6] has influenced storytelling with his particular method of biblical storytelling. His method does not use eye contact, but does use simple figures as props. "Wondering" questions after the story are essential to the process.

Each teacher needs to use a method that feels comfortable. Props such as flannel boards or pictures are quite appropriate. Some stories are more conducive to one style or another and suggestions are made in the curriculum itself. However, each teacher needs to be creative and adapt the stories so that the children listen and learn from the storytelling process.

7. Personal History of Abuse

Many teachers find that their own personal history impacts their ability to teach this course to children. Some teachers find that their own experiences make it hard to talk about child sexual abuse. Others find that their history is a primary motivation for helping children. It is essential that every teacher find support for himself or herself during this course. Teaching this class as a team is ideal. Pastors and other teachers can be very supportive of the adults teaching this course.

More and more religious educators are aware of the importance of sexual abuse prevention. Any leaders who have new ideas or creative uses for ideas and activities are asked to share their experience by writing to the Center for the Prevention of Sexual and Domestic Violence, 1914 N. 34th St., Suite 105, Seattle, Washington 98103.

Overcoming Church Resistance

Although many parents and church leaders are concerned about child sexual abuse, resistance to teaching child abuse prevention in the church is common. Some parents worry that their children will receive too much explicit information about sexuality; others think that perhaps their children will become fearful of others and worry about evil. However, children without information and resources have few defenses against those who seek to harm them.

The most important factor in overcoming resistance in a church is the pastor's support for child abuse prevention. The more a congregation has heard about this issue and other related issues of domestic violence, the more receptive it will be to having a prevention program. Pastors who frequently preach on domestic violence, who openly discuss violence against women and children, and who support programs that help survivors are laying the groundwork for a congregation's support.

Even if the pastor has not taken a lead in the past, pastoral support is important for anyone proposing child sexual abuse prevention in the religious education program. The pastor can show support by talking about the program and the need for it in sermons. The pastor can also be an advocate in congregational education committees. Pastoral support can help overcome parents' fear.

Another way to overcome resistance is for parents to request a child sexual abuse prevention program for their children. An advocate for this kind of program can talk to parents and others about the availability of materials and the willingness of teachers. Oftentimes when concerned parents learn about the curriculum or hear of other children getting information, they too want this program for their children.

Finally, church education committees need to be educated about the need for this kind of material. They need information about how the curriculum works and its purpose. Quite often after they have been asked to examine the curriculum and look at supplemental resources, they are also convinced that child abuse prevention is necessary.

Preparing the Church for the Curriculum

An important task for teachers of this curriculum is to prepare the church for using these materials in church school classes. Many churches have not had the opportunity to discuss and learn about child sexual abuse. Therefore, the adult leaders need to introduce the topic to the parents and the entire congregation.

The congregation can be prepared by having announcements in newsletters and bulletins about the future use of these materials. Some churches find that it is a great opportunity to have an adult education class before or even during the use of this material with children. Finally, the pastor and other leaders of the church can make public and private affirmations that support the use of this material.

Parents' Meetings

Although most parents are appreciative of having child sexual abuse prevention materials available to their children in a church school setting, some parents have concerns or would like more details about the materials. Before this course begins, parents and other adults in the church can have an opportunity to look at the materials and learn more about them. This is also an opportunity to show parents books and videos that will help them understand child sexual abuse.

It is strongly recommended that the leaders arrange to meet with parents and other interested adults. This provides an opportunity for parents to be educated first and alerted to some of the material their children will be learning. Parents will then be better prepared to respond to the questions and concerns their children voice. Such a meeting also provides an opportunity for parents to raise any questions about the content of the course. A clear explanation of what will be presented usually addresses the concerns and minimizes resistance. Appendix A contains an information sheet on sexual abuse that can be copied and handed out.

Parents should not attend sessions with children. Some children may be reluctant to discuss sexual abuse in front of their parents. Each session contains a "For You to Take Home" sheet. This sheet includes information about the session's objectives and also has an activity for the child to do at home. This sheet can be a way for adults and children to begin to discuss issues concerning child sexual abuse. An explanation of this, when made at the parents' meeting, is usually understood by parents. If the parents have enough interest, a parents' class on the same topic might be offered.

Sample Parent Letter

Dear Parent,

Increasingly, parents are concerned about their children's safety. In particular, sexual abuse is a great concern to parents. The statistics are staggering. One out of every three girls and one out of every seven boys will be molested before the age of eighteen. Each year over 100,000 young people are sexually assaulted in our country. [Name of church] is committed to being a community that cares for children. Therefore, we are providing several opportunities for families to learn more about how to prevent sexual assault.

During the next months, [name of church school class] will be studying a special church school curriculum on preventing child sexual abuse. As parents concerned about the safety of your children, we want you to be informed about all aspects of this program. We are providing a Christian education program that teaches children about God's constant care, trains children to recognize and deal with potentially dangerous situations, and teaches children about resources in our community and within our church to help children who have been hurt.

In addition to the Sunday morning classes for the children, we are offering a workshop on [date] at [time] for parents and other interested adults. This workshop will include information on child sexual abuse, communication tips on talking to your child, and a description of the children's classes.

You are urged to attend this adult workshop. Your questions or concerns could be helpful to us. We hope that you will encourage your child to participate in church school class during [dates]. If you are unable to attend the adult workshop and you have questions concerning this unit, please feel free to call me.

Sincerely,

Phone #:

Dealing with Younger Children and Our Fears

As I discuss child abuse prevention with parents and teachers in the church, it seems that my personal story, as a parent accused of child abuse, relieves parental fears and helps them understand some of the issues. My greatest fear, of course, has been that my children will experience child abuse. I have always wanted to keep them safe. However, I believe that every parent worries that somehow prevention education may have an adverse effect on his or her child and their family. In addition, many parents fear that some experience within the family will be misinterpreted as abuse.

In 1985, my youngest child, Jesse, attended a full-day preschool sponsored by our local public school. I was completing my seminary degree and working as an associate pastor. My husband was teaching full-time at the seminary. Jesse was in his second year of preschool, headed for kindergarten in the fall. The preschool curriculum included a Child Abuse Prevention Program, which he had attended. Overall, he loved school. His teachers experienced him as an energetic and imaginative child.

One afternoon during recess, he found an especially appealing large ball of used bubble gum that he picked up and chewed. Later during nap time, he stretched the gum and created a bubble-gum mask that he stuck over his eyes. By the time he returned home that evening, he had bubble gum and dirt stuck around his eyes and looked like a raccoon. His father and I worked on removing the gum, but we found that rubbing the gum off made it look even worse because we were literally rubbing the skin off with the gum. I remember quite clearly telling Jesse that we had done all we could for one day and that we would try again the next day. We also discussed in detail the hazards of chewing used bubble gum.

The next day, the school nurse came checking for lice and notice Jesse's eyes. The morning staff of the preschool could not explain what had happened. When asked, Jesse told the school nurse that he had gotten these "black eyes" from a beating by his dad. This story continued in the school principal's office, where he added that we routinely beat him with a belt, hung him out the window, and threw him down the stairs.

By 10:30 A.M., a Child Protective Services investigator was on my door asking questions. He interviewed both my husband and me and asked about how we disciplined our children. He looked through the house for evidence that we had in fact done what Jesse had described. Finally, he explained the investigation that would follow.

I had just started learning about child abuse in classes at the seminary and elsewhere and knew how serious these accusations were. I wondered whether people would believe us and whether we could prove our innocence. My husband and I felt a range of emotions, from pure anger to fear that our family would be separated and destroyed.

The good news was that Jesse was to be returned to the family that afternoon, because, as the investigator told us, Jesse had giggled and laughed, showing no fear of his home as he described his abuse. Jesse's older brothers and sister were to be interviewed at school in the coming days. Jesse's older brother, age 13, experienced anger and resentment about the possibility that our family could be separated.

Although the investigation lasted only one week and we were cleared of all charges, I felt incredible shame about being investigated. I shared my experience with a close friend, who was also the senior pastor at the church where I worked. I also called the Center for Prevention of Domestic and Sexual Violence in order to allow them to disassociate themselves from me and the accusations. I had nightmares that I could wake to newspaper stories and that my friends would not understand.

As time went on, I began to realize that I needed to tell this story. Other parents and teachers needed to hear about my experience. Oftentimes we make assumptions about how the system fails or the guilt/innocence of the accused. Seldom do we have all the facts and information. As a church school teacher and pastor, I am responsible for reporting information about possible child abuse. I am not the investigator.

In my case, my son appeared to be abused and the school nurse cared enough about children to report what she had observed to Child Protective Services. The investigator was competent and able to sort through the physical evidence and information to make a determination about the accusations.

Although I felt great shame, our family was able to turn this experience into the basis for more prevention education within our family. All of us were able to talk about what abuse is and how it happens in families. In the end, I decided that I would rather risk an accusation than have someone see signs of abuse in my child and fail to report. I'm glad the school nurse cared enough to report.

It has taken a long time for us to process this experience, and we still talk about it today. The anger is gone, but I know a parent's fear of having his or her family destroyed. My husband and I needed to work on our feelings toward Jesse. We had to learn to talk with him about abuse even as he continued to threaten to report us for making him clean his room.

Perhaps my greatest sadness comes from knowing that while the system worked for me, it does not always work for others. More than a year later I was able to talk to Jesse about where he got the idea of telling the nurse about being beaten with a belt. It was then that he told me about the little boy who slept on the mat next to him at nap time. This little boy suffered all the abuse that Jesse described, but he was not able to tell anyone who could help him. I know now that in Jesse's own way, he was trying to help by telling adults about the abuse that was happening in this boy's life.

Session 1
God Cares About Children

Objectives

- To increase the children's awareness that God values children.
- To empower the children so that they can try to protect themselves by saying "no" to a potentially abusive situation.
- To help children understand child abuse.

Theological and Biblical Concepts

The story of Samuel (1 Samuel 3:1–19) is about a boy who hears the voice of God. Not only does God speak directly to this child, but God also entrusts an important message to him.

In the Hebrew Scriptures' world of priests and prophets, Samuel is chosen by God. As he lies in his bed at night, he hears a voice that he mistakes as the voice of Eli, the priest. Finally Samuel understands that God has a special message for him to tell Eli and the people.

In our society as well as in ancient times, many adults would question whether children are capable of hearing the voice of God. Few people would believe a child who tells others about hearing the voice of God. Some would even argue that children are not responsible or mature enough for God to entrust them with an important message. Yet this biblical text reminds us that God valued Samuel and spoke directly to him.

Even though Samuel is only one child, he remains an example of the value of children in the eyes of God. God speaks to adults, and God also speaks directly to children. This is one of the ways that we know God values children.

Because children are special, they have rights. They have the rights to shelter, food, clothing, education. Children's rights include the right to say "no" to an adult who wants to abuse a child. Many times saying "no" does not stop the abuse from happening. It is very important to tell the children that abuse is not his or her fault whether the child has said "no" or not.

Resources Needed

Name tags and markers
Chalk and chalkboard or newsprint and markers
Copies of "For You to Take Home" page and Activity Sheet 1

Teacher Preparation

1. Read 1 Samuel 3:1–19 and Matthew 19:14. Learn the stories so that you can tell them with enthusiasm and meaning. The story is very exciting for younger children. Emphasize that God chose to speak directly to a child. If you don't have time to learn the story, practice reading it so that you can keep the children's interest as you read. (See the note in the Introduction about storytelling.)
2. Review the entire lesson.
3. Make copies of "For You to Take Home" page.
4. Learn the song.

NOTE TO THE TEACHER

Throughout this course, information will be written on chalkboards and charts. In order to help the children review and to keep the flow of information, it is a good idea to make charts that can be kept to use throughout of the course. These charts can be good tools to use in review information in future sessions.

This Session in Brief

Getting Started (10 min)

Introduce the Course
Set Ground Rules

Developing the Session

Samuel Hears the Voice of God (15 min)
Rights (10 min)
What Is Child Abuse? (15 min)

Concluding the Session (10 min)

Summarize and Evaluate
Invite Questions
Closing

The Session Plan

Getting Started

Introduce the Course

- Begin class by introducing yourself. You may know some of the children and their families through your experience of teaching or other roles that you have in the church.
- Pass out markers and name tags explaining that we need to be able to call each person by her/his name. The teacher may need to help some children print their names.
- Ask each person to introduce himself or herself to the group. If you are new to the children or there are visitors present, ask the children to give the group information about themselves.
- Explain that the topic of this special church school class will be how to keep people from hurting them and what to do if someone does hurt them. This course will be about a special kind of child abuse: child sexual abuse. Ask the children if they know anything about the topic. Listen carefully to their responses because many children already have ideas, some accurate and some inaccurate. Some school systems include sexual abuse prevention materials in the early elementary grades. Ask the children how many of them have had a special class at school. Explain that the church is supposed to be a place for help and healing. Therefore it is a good place to learn more about protecting yourself and what to do if you need help. Explain that everyone will have lots of chances to ask questions about this topic.

Set Ground Rules

- Explain that asking questions is important.
- Remind the children that listening carefully to each person is important so that everyone understands what is being said.
- Tell the children that the teachers are available between sessions to talk about anything in this course.

NOTE TO THE TEACHER

One advantage to having a team teach this material is that with more than one teacher in the classroom, one teacher is available to pay attention immediately to a child while the other teacher can continue the lesson. It is also very important that trusted adults are available for children between sessions and after the sessions. Teachers may give the children their home phone numbers.

Developing the Session

Samuel Hears the Voice of God

Tell the story of Samuel's hearing the voice of God from 1 Samuel 3:1–19.

- Explain that in ancient times, children were thought of as property. Children had no rights. Less than a hundred years ago, children had no rights in this country. Often children had to work long hours in factories and in the fields, because they helped to support their families.
- God spoke to Samuel and gave him a very special message.
- All children are special to God.
- Every child has God-given rights.

NOTE TO THE TEACHER

Many church school classes will be ongoing classes that have been together for most of the school year. Other classes, however, will be newly formed for this course. Classes that have been together for a longer time do not need much time to get acquainted. New classes need more time before plunging into this material. If the class is newly formed, it is suggested that the teacher insert a get-acquainted game or short activity to help children meet one another. Assign partners and have each child ask the other to share three things that are then, in turn, shared with the group.

Rights

Define for the children what rights are: Rights are the things that are yours because you are a person.

Lead a discussion about the rights of children.

- What are rights of children?
- List the rights of children. (Use a chalkboard and chalk or newsprint and markers.)
- Compare the children's list of rights with this list:

You have the right to:
food
shelter
clothing
education
love
live free from fear
be safe

Explain that this means that children should have all of these things and should not be kept from any of them. The teacher can write these rights on a poster to keep up during the entire class.

- Tell the children the story of Jesus and the children in Matthew 19:14. Explain that in this story the parents brought their children so that Jesus could bless the children, but the disciples thought that Jesus had more important work to do and stopped the children from getting close to Jesus. Jesus told the disciples, "Let the children come to me; do not try to stop them; for the dominion of Heaven belongs to such as these." And Jesus laid his hands on the children.

Explain that Jesus was telling the disciples how each child is important to God. Because each child is loved by God, no child should be kept from any of the things on our list of rights.

- These rights include the right to say "no" if an adult asks you to do something that gives you fear or makes you feel unsafe.

In what situations do children need to say "no!"? Ask the children for ideas. Here are some:

- When someone wants a child to take drugs
- When someone wants a child to commit a crime
- When someone wants a child to hurt another person
- When an adult wants a child to touch his or her private parts
  (private parts are anything covered by a bathing suit)
- When an adult or an older child wants to touch a child's private parts
- When an adult wants a child to take off their clothing to pose for pictures

What Is Child Abuse?

The adult leader should lead a discussion with the children about child abuse.

- What is child abuse?
- Have any children ever seen anything about child abuse on television?
- Has anyone ever known anyone who experienced child abuse?

Explain that there are different kinds of child abuse:
1. **Physical abuse** is when an adult or older child (teenager or child more than several years older) hurts a child by hurting the child's body. Examples: hitting, pinching, burning, or shaking a child.
2. **Emotional and verbal abuse** is when an adult or older child hurts a child by saying things that make the child feel bad about himself or herself. Examples: calling people names or making a child feel like nothing is good about him or her.
3. **Physical neglect** is when an adult or older child does not take good care of a child. Examples: not feeding or clothing a child, letting the child be unsafe, or not taking a sick child to the doctor.
4. **Sexual abuse**. Touching a child's private parts or asking a child to touch an adult's or older child's private parts. Session 4 will be about this kind of abuse.

NOTE TO THE TEACHER

Child abuse is defined as an adult or older child hurting a child, physically, emotionally, or sexually. An older child could be a teenager or another child more than three years older. Each state has different legal definitions about what the age gap must be for prosecution of the abuse. However, any sexual activity in which another child is physically larger or mentally more able to trick or force another child, no matter what the age difference, should be considered abuse. Children who are mentally disabled are often the victims of child abuse by adults and other children.

Emphasize that child abuse is against the law because it hurts children. It is also against God's will. Children have the right to be safe. God does not want children to be hurt. Tell the children that it is never the child's fault. It is always the adult or older child's fault for the abuse.

Emphasize that rights are God's gift to every person. They are something to which every human being is entitled.

BACKGROUND FOR THE TEACHER

Most adults and children tend to think that child abuse is physical endangerment only; however, it is important that child abuse be understood to include much more than physical implications:

Physical abuse and corporal punishment resulting in a traumatic condition
Emotional and verbal abuse
Physical neglect and/or inadequate supervision
Sexual abuse and exploitation

Call the local Child Abuse Council or consult other local sources about the laws regarding child abuse in your area.

NOTE FOR THE TEACHER

For younger children, keep words and definitions simple. Children are able to understand the different kinds of child abuse if the definitions are simple and the examples clear. Be prepared for children to ask specific questions about whether or not a specific action (e.g., spanking) is abusive. Help the children understand that abuse is much more than being unhappy. Being displeased with parents or not getting a wish is not abuse.

Concluding the Session

Summarize and Review

Gather the children together for a time to share discoveries made in this session. Describe plans for the next session.

Remind the children that the teachers are available after each session to talk to anyone. Once again, give the children a home phone number where they may reach the teacher during the week.

Invite Questions

Always take time to answer any questions the children have. Tell them that their parents have received a letter about this class. Suggest that they might want to find a trusted adult, perhaps a parent or someone else, to talk about the topics that are discussed in this course. Give each child a "For You to Take Home" page.

Closing

Introduce the song printed on Activity Sheet 1. This song can be a theme song for the entire course. Use the song in the introduction or closing of any session.

The song is especially appropriate for younger children as it can be sung antiphonally. The leader might sing the first phrase and children would then "sing it back." This works very well with younger children who cannot read.

Discuss the ideas in the song with the children. They can also make up appropriate movements to the words in the song.

Activity Sheet 1

Shout for God!

Words by Walter Farquharson, Music by Ron Klusmeier, Cascade, Wisc.: Worship Arts–Resources for Ministry, 1986, *Just Like Salt*, p. 66.

For You to Take Home

In today's session we learned:

- God spoke to Samuel.
- Some children are hurt by adults or older children. We call that child abuse.
- Children have rights, including the right to say "no" to an adult or older child who wants them to do something that is wrong.

Here's an activity to do at home.

Code Message

Long ago Samuel heard the voice of God. God talked directly to Samuel in the night. At first, he thought it was the priest, Eli, calling him. But God had a message for Samuel. God cared about Samuel.

To find the message below, you must write the correct letter under each umber. The key will tell you which letter to write.

7 15 4   3 1 18 5 19   1 2 15 21 20   25 15 21   20 15 15

__ __ __   __ __ __ __ __   __ __ __ __ __   __ __ __   __ __ __.

Key

1 = A	8 = H	15 = O	22 = V
2 = B	9 = I	16 = P	23 = W
3 = C	10 = J	17 = Q	24 = X
4 = D	11 = K	18 = R	25 = Y
5 = E	12 = L	19 = S	26 = Z
6 = F	13 = M	20 = T	
7 = G	14 = N	21 = U	

CODE MESSAGE: God cares about you too.

Session 2

God Created Me!

Objectives

- To increase children's understanding that all people, both male and female, are created in God's image as bodily beings.
- To increase children's understanding that their bodies belong to them.
- To help children recognize appropriate and inappropriate touch.

Theological and Biblical Concepts

In Genesis 1:26–31, God's creation is declared as good. Human beings are part of that creation and are also affirmed as good. All too often, we forget that the goodness of creation includes our bodies as well as our minds and spirits. Our bodies are part of God's creation. This session teaches children that they are unique creations of God and that God loves them. Our bodies belong to us. Our bodies are to be cared for as part of God's creation.

Resources Needed

Newsprint or chalkboard
Copies of Activity Sheets 2 and 3
Copies of "For You to Take Home" page
Crayons and markers for drawing pictures
Poster with "Touching Safety Rules"
Blank newsprint for optional drawing activity

Teacher Preparation

1. Read Genesis 1:26–31. Learn the story so that you can tell it with enthusiasm and meaning. This does not mean that you must memorize the story; you certainly may use notes. If you don't have time to learn the story, practice reading it so that you can keep the children's interest as you read. (See the note about storytelling in the introduction.)
2. Review the entire lesson. Learn the games.

3. Make copies of Activity Sheets 2 and 3 and "For You to Take Home" page.

4. Make a poster with the "Touching Safety Rules" (see Activity Sheet 3). Keep this poster on the wall for the entire course. Session 6 uses this poster again.

Session in Brief

Getting Started

Building Community (10 min)
Questions and Answers

Developing the Session

Each Child Is Special (10 min)
Activity: Memory Game
God's Creation Is Good (15 min)
Activity
Optional Activity
My Body Belongs to Me! (15 min)
Additional Bible Study

Concluding the Session (10 min)

Summarize and Evaluate
Closing

The Session Plan

Getting Started

Building Community

- Begin this session by asking the children about something that they remember from the last session.

Questions and Answers

- Answer any questions that the children might have.

Developing the Session

Each Child Is Special

Ask the children if it is possible for two people to be <u>exactly</u> alike. Many of the children will say that twins can be alike. Tell them that even twins are not exactly alike. Even identical twins are a little different. Some twins like different kinds of music or get different grades in school. Each person is special and unique.

Activity: Memory Game

- Ask the children to count off by 2s and form a circle.
- Form an inner circle by asking the "1"s to step into the center and face a "2."
- Give the inner circle 30 seconds to memorize everything about the person facing them. Instruct them to look carefully at faces, clothing, jewelry, etc.
- Ask the children who memorized to turn their backs for a few seconds so that others can change two things about themselves.
- Have the inner circle turn around and try to guess what the person facing them has changed.
- Let the outer circle have a turn.

Take a few minutes to discuss with the children what they learned from the memory game.

- What changes were easy to notice?
- What changes were hard to notice?
- When you first see a person, what do you notice first?
- Name two ways in which you and your partner are similar.
- Name two ways in which you are different.
- Everyone has some things the same, name some of them.
- Everyone has some things that are different, name some of them.

God's Creation Is Good

Tell the children about the creation account in Genesis 1:26–31. Look at the verses on the "For You to Take Home" page. Discuss this passage.

Notice that humans are an important part of the creation story.
Point out that males and females are made in the image of God. That means girls and boys are both made in the image of God.
God declares that all of the creation, including humans, is good.

NOTE TO THE TEACHER

It is important that teachers be sensitive to children with disabilities during this activity; they have the same feelings about their bodies as other children. However, social pressure is even more likely to make these children feel bad about their bodies. Teachers should emphasize that all people are made in God's image, and everyone likes some parts of his or her body. Do not ignore differences, but stress the things all children have in common. Depending on the kinds of disabilities present in your setting, you will want to adjust activities accordingly.

Ask children to name one thing that they like about their body; for example:

- What do you like about your feet?
- What about your hands?
- Name a good thing about your face.

NOTE TO THE TEACHER

Even though a child can understand that his or her body belongs to him or her, it is important that the children also understand that human beings are not a form of property. Emphasize that even though you "own" your body, it is not something that can be sold or given away.

Activity

Give each child a copy of Activity Sheet 2 on which to draw a picture of his or her whole self. The children should be encouraged to draw themselves anyway they choose. Pay attention to the details that they include. Keep these papers for sharing in Session 4.

Optional Activity

Use blank newsprint to draw a full-size silhouette of each child. Ask each child to lie down on the paper and outline them with a marker. Then have each child draw facial features, hair, clothing, and shoes to make the paper child look just like themselves.

Put these silhouettes up around the room. Ask the class to walk around, look at each picture, and say aloud (or silently), "Thank you, God for [name of child]."

NOTE TO THE TEACHER

Drawing a picture of themselves at this age may take the children only a few minutes. Some children may be reluctant to draw themselves. It might be useful to have the children draw pictures while continuing the discussion. Another idea is to play music while the children draw. This may also help the children relax.

If a child has such low self-esteem that she or he cannot make an affirming statement about him- or herself and draws a very negative image, encourage the child to tell you about the characteristic or aspect of him- or herself that she or he likes best.

"My Body Belongs to Me!"

Ask the children to name the parts of a person's body: legs, hands, arms, etc. Some may even name private parts like "bottom," "booty," "wee-wee." Expect them to include some of these parts. They may be testing you, so do not show any embarrassment. If slang terms are suggested for body parts, ask the children if they know the correct term. If they don't, tell them. Be sure to use correct terms: penis, breast, bottom, etc.

Ask if they know what "private parts" are. If they don't know, suggest that private parts are the parts of the body that are covered by a swimsuit or by underwear. Explain that it is not okay for an adult or an older child to touch a child's private parts except for health and safety reasons. Even if the adult or older child is a family member or someone a child loves, it is not okay to touch a child's private parts. Explain that it is not okay for an adult or older child to ask a child to touch the adult's or older child's private parts.

Explain to the children that there are times when touching is appropriate. We call these "health and safety reasons." Ask the children to give some examples of when it is okay to touch private parts.

- Doctors with a nurse or parent present
- Parents in special situations (e.g., bathing)
- When you wash yourself

Explain that our bodies are our gift to explore.

- It is okay to touch yourself.
- It is important to take care of yourself.
- You are responsible for self-care.

Explain that it is NEVER okay for a grown-up to touch a child's private parts if the grown-up makes it a secret. Tell the children that their body belongs to them. Hand out Activity Sheet 3. (An optional activity is to color this picture.)

Have a chart with the "Touching Safety Rules" from Activity Sheet 3 for the children to see. Ask the children to repeat these rules after the teacher. Help the children remember the rules.

- It is never okay for a grown-up or older child to touch a child's private parts and make it a secret.
- It is not okay for a grown-up or older child to ask a child to touch the grown-up's private parts.

Additional Bible Study

Read Psalms 8:3–5 (on the "For You to Take Home" sheet) about the goodness of the creation of humans. Discuss this passage. Notice that humans are called "little less than God." Point out that the passage says that humans are so important to God that God remembers and cares for them.

Concluding the Session

Summarize and Evaluate

Ask the children to share some ideas learned and feelings about what happened in the session.

Tell the children about future sessions.

Remind the children that the teachers are available after each session to talk to anyone. Once again, give the children a home phone number where they may reach the teacher during the week.

Closing

For a closing, the class will have a litany. Ask the group to say, "God made me, too," after each sentence that the teacher says.

(Children can make motions with each line the teacher says. As the children say their line, ask them to point to themselves.)

Teacher: *God made the fish of the sea. [Make fish motion with hands]*

Children: God made me, too.

Teacher: *God made the birds of the air. [Form flying birds with hands]*

Children: God made me, too.

Teacher: *God made the cattle and the wild animals. [Make wild animal sounds like growling.]*

Children: God made me, too.

Teacher: *God made the creeping animals on the earth. [Make spider with hands.]*

Children: God made me, too.

Teacher: God made girls. [Point to girls.]
Children: God made me, too.
Teacher: God made boys. [Point to boys.]
Children: God made me, too.
Teacher: God made our bodies. [Grab your toes.]
Children: God made me, too.
Teacher: And God's creation is good. [Stretch out arms.]
Children: God made me, too.
Teacher: Amen.

NOTE TO THE TEACHER

It is important that you always remember that chances are very good that your class will have a child who is or has been sexually abused. This study guide is written to help children protect themselves, and it is possible that a child might disclose personal or a friend's abuse. Every session should include an invitation to disclose this abuse privately. The children should be reminded that the teacher is available and that there are also trusted adults who will want to talk to them.

Activity Sheet 2

This is a picture of me!

I am special to God!

Activity Sheet 3

- It is never okay for a grown-up or older child to touch a child's private parts and make it a secret.
- It is not okay for a grown-up or older child to ask a child to touch the grown-up's private parts.

For You to Take Home

In today's session we learned:

- God created people, both male and female, in God's image.
- My body belongs to me.
- Rules to help protect us against child abuse.
- I can recognize appropriate and inappropriate touch.

These are some of the scriptures that I learned about:

So God created humankind in God's image, in the image of God created them; male and female God created them. And God saw everything that God had made, and behold it was very good. And there was evening and there was morning, a sixth day. [Genesis 1:27 and 31, NRSV]

When I look at your heavens, the work of your fingers,
the moon and the stars which you have established;
what are human beings that you are mindful of them,
and mortals that you care for them?
Yet you have made them little less than God,
and crowned them with glory and honor.
[Psalm 8:3–5]

This is a page that I can color at home.

Session 3

Why Do Bad Things Happen to People?

Objectives

- To expand children's understanding that bad things sometimes happen to us and those we love.
- To increase participants' awareness that God gives us choices in life.
- To increase the children's awareness that God is always present with us.

Theological and Biblical Concepts

Generations of Christians have struggled to understand why innocent people suffer greatly. Everyone has wondered why someone has been hurt, a tragedy happened, or a natural disaster occurred. Although some bad things that happen seem to be unexplainable, others are the direct result of someone doing evil. Hurricanes, earthquakes, and storms that kill people are natural disasters. Car and airplane crashes are accidents. Wars, murder, and abuse are examples of bad things caused by human behavior and choices.

In Deuteronomy, Moses addresses the kinds of choices that human beings have. He explains that people have a choice between good and evil, life and death. He begins by reviewing God's saving acts, but reminds the people that they are at a critical time in history when important decisions must be made. The choices that face the people of God will determine their future.

Although written for a specific group of people, chapter 30, verses 15–20, also remind us of the importance of choices. Moses makes a clear and simple statement about good and evil. We know that life is more complex and that choices are often difficult. However, each person makes choices daily between good and evil. These choices we make not only influence our future but also affect the well being of others. Many of the bad things that happen in our world are due to many wrong choices. Abuse happens because offenders make choices that harm others.

Although we do not understand why things happen in our world, we can be assured that God does not cause these bad things to happen, nor do survivors of child abuse deserve the abuse they receive. As we struggle with why bad things happen to good people, we need to remember that God's presence and love are with us, even when we suffer.

Teacher Preparation

1. Write Genesis 30:15–20 on a newsprint so that the entire class can look at the words as you read the passage to them.
2. Review the entire lesson. Gather needed supplies.
3. One activity in this session is making puppets. The puppets can be used in acting out future Bible stories and also in role-playing or puppet shows. Cut out felt bodies of the puppets so that the group members can glue them together and decorate them. (An alternative method of putting the puppets together is to stitch 1/4 inch around the outside of the puppet. Turn the puppet so that the seam is on the inside.)
4. Collect fabric scraps and markers to decorate the puppets.

Resources Needed

Newsprint and markers, or chalkboard and chalk
Copies of Activity Sheet 4 and "For You to Take Home" page
Two (8-1/2 by 11 inches) pieces of felt for each student
Glue
Yarn, fabric scraps, rickrack, hem tape, or other decorations
Permanent markers, fabric markers, or liquid embroidery
Puppet pattern on Activity Sheet 5

This Session in Brief

Getting Started (10 min)

Build Community
Questions and Answers

Developing the Session (40 min)

List Bad Things
Bible Study
Making Puppets

Concluding the Session (10 min)

Summarize and Evaluate
Closing

The Session Plan

Getting Started

Build Community

Describe briefly the plan for the session today. Take a few minutes to ask each child what they remember from the previous sessions.

Questions and Answers

Answer any questions that the children have.

Developing the Session

List Bad Things

On newsprint or a chalkboard, make a list of bad things that happen to people:

hurricanes
tornadoes
homelessness
getting beat up
being sick
car wreck
death
pet hit by a car
children starving
airplane crashes

Discuss this list with the children.

- What makes these things bad? (People are hurt and experience pain or loss.)
- Have you or someone you know ever experienced these things?
- Which ones?
- What is the difference between these things?

Make three columns on a separate sheet:

- Natural disasters/illness
- Accidents
- Harm done by someone to another

Take the first list and put each item under one of the three columns. Discuss each category and why these bad things happen.

Natural Disasters/Illness: Some things just happen. For example, natural forces of weather come together in ways that create storms that sometimes hurt people. Illness is caused by germs that can make us sick; sometimes we pass those germs on to someone else and they get sick. Tornadoes are caused by warm and cold air meeting; God does not make tornadoes.

Accidents: Accidents often happen because someone was careless or made a mistake. A car wreck might occur if someone isn't paying attention while driving and runs a red light or stop sign. Sometimes someone will be hurt or killed because someone else was careless or thoughtless.

Harm Done by Someone: Some people in the world hurt other people on purpose. They do things that are scary and harmful to children. They like to be in charge. They like to make people do what they want them to do. We call these people "abusers."

Remind the children that unfortunately many abusers were hurt themselves when they were children. No one was there to protect them or love them, and now they have chosen to turn their hurt onto other people. But this is their choice. They can also choose not to hurt anyone else. Other responsible adults must help abusers learn not to hurt others.

Bible Study

Read Genesis 30:15–20 to the class and discuss the scripture:

- Moses says that there are two types of choices, what are they?
- What happens when people make good choices?
- What happens when people made bad choices?

NOTE TO THE TEACHER

In Genesis, Moses makes the choice straightforward, clear, and simple. The people are asked to choose between good and evil, life and death. Although we know that life is more complex, children need to understand that making the wrong choices can result in hurting others.

Show the class the three categories of bad things and ask them children: Where is God in all of these bad things? Remind them that God doesn't cause bad things to happen. God does not like it when bad things happen to us.

Ask the class: Why do some people do bad things? Remind them that God allows us to make choices even when we make bad choices that hurt other people. God would rather we make good choices that don't hurt other people.

Also tell the children that when someone makes a bad choice and hurts someone else, God promises always to be there to comfort. God will never desert us when bad things happen. God is also there for the person who causes the hurt. God wants that person never to hurt anyone again.

NOTE TO THE TEACHER

A resource for teachers is the book *When Bad Things Happen to Good People*, by Harold S. Kushner (New York: Avon Books, 1981).

Making Puppets

Give each group member a felt puppet to glue together and then decorate. Puppets can be male or female, young or old. These puppets will be used in later sessions, so ask the children to leave their puppets in the classroom for future use.

Concluding the Session

Summarize and Evaluate

Spend a few minutes recalling what has happened during the session. Answer any questions about this session and give the children some ideas about what will happen in future sessions.

Remind the children that the teachers are available after each session to talk. Once again give the children a home phone number where they may reach the teacher during the week.

Closing

Ask the children either to stand or sit in a circle and to pray together the reflective prayer on Activity Sheet 4.

Activity Sheet 4

Prayer

Dear God,

We do not always understand why bad things happen. People are hurt by hurricanes, earthquakes, and tornadoes. People get sick and have diseases. People are hurt by other people. Some children live in countries where there is war. Sometimes a big person hurts a child. Sometimes people make bad choices that harm others.

We know that you do not cause these things to happen. You stay with us during good things and bad things that happen to us. Help us to make good choices. Thank you for being our friend.

Activity Sheet 5

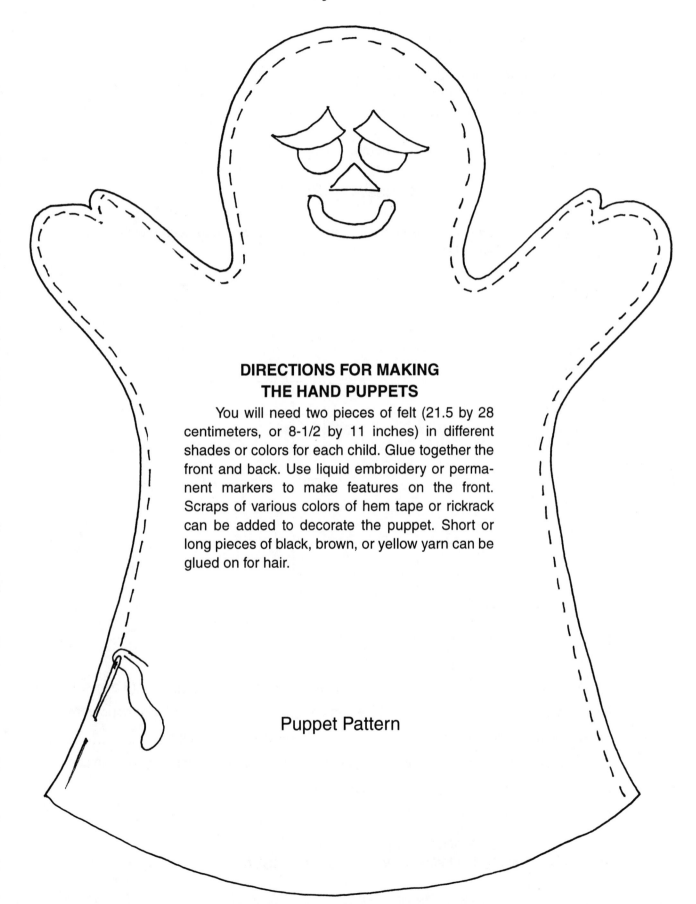

DIRECTIONS FOR MAKING THE HAND PUPPETS

You will need two pieces of felt (21.5 by 28 centimeters, or 8-1/2 by 11 inches) in different shades or colors for each child. Glue together the front and back. Use liquid embroidery or permanent markers to make features on the front. Scraps of various colors of hem tape or rickrack can be added to decorate the puppet. Short or long pieces of black, brown, or yellow yarn can be glued on for hair.

Puppet Pattern

For You to Take Home

In today's session we learned:

- Bad things happen to people.
- God gives each of us choices.
- God is with us even when bad things happen.

Here's an activity that we can do at home.

Crossword Puzzle

See if you can put words from today's scripture into the crossword puzzle. (If you need help, use the word list.)

Word List

bad
things
like
choices
make
people
happen

God doesn't cause _____ (2 across) things to _____ (3 across). God doesn't _____ (7 down) it when bad _____ (5 across) happen to us. But God allows us to make _____ (4 down) even when we _____ (1 down) bad choices that hurt other people. God would rather we make good choices that don't hurt other _____ (6 across).

ANSWERS: Across—(2) bad; (3) happen; (5) things; (6) people. Down—(1) make; (4) choices; (7) like.

Session 4
God Wants Me to Be Safe

Objectives

- To expand the children's image of God to include God as a source of comfort.
- To help children understand child sexual abuse.

Theological and Biblical Concepts

As a source of comfort, God has been compared to a shepherd. Jesus begins talking about power and the value of children. In Matthew 18:10–14, Jesus uses the metaphor of God as a shepherd who searches diligently for the one lost sheep. In some Christian traditions, this scripture is only taught as a metaphor of God seeking out sinners or sheep who have strayed from the fold. However, anyone who experiences the feelings of being alone, separated from God and others, or being hurt by others knows what if feels like to be the lost sheep. The lost sheep could be anyone who experiences any kind of hurt. Children who have experienced child abuse may feel they are separated from others, including members of their own family. They may feel like the lost sheep. In this scripture, the image of God as a shepherd presents God as a source of comfort.

In Matthew 23:37, Jesus uses the metaphor of God being a mother hen who gathers her brood under her wing. This image of God as a mother hen also presents God as a source of comfort.

For children, the images of God as a shepherd or as a mother hen can be a source of healing and comfort. These images are very important to those who have experienced some kind of hurt. God desires that people be safe and cared for. Not only is child abuse against the law, it is against what God wants for children.

Resources Needed

Newsprint or chalkboard
Markers or chalk
Copies of Activity Sheet 6 and "For You to Take Home" sheet
Watercolors or other nontoxic paints
Figures for telling the story

Teacher Preparation

1. Read Matthew 18:10–14. Learn the parable so that you can tell the story with enthusiasm and meaning. This story is especially suited to be told with small figures to illustrate it. Use a cloth to make the hills, some plain wooden blocks to be the corral for the sheep, and a simple wooden figure to be the shepherd. You can use cotton balls to be the sheep. (See the note in the introduction about storytelling.)
2. Review the entire lesson.
3. Make copies of Activity Sheet 4 and "For You to Take Home" sheet.

This Session in Brief

Getting Started (10 min)

Building Community
Questions and Answers

Developing the Session

Review
Sexual Abuse: A Special Kind of Child Abuse (10 min)
God as a Shepherd/Mother Hen (10 min)
Learn Ways to Protect Yourself (10 min)
Activity: "What If" Game (10 min)
Art Activity

Concluding the Session (10 min)

Summarize and Evaluate
Closing

The Session Plan

Getting Started

Building Community

Ask each child to share the picture that he or she drew of him- or herself in Session 2. If they don't feel comfortable sharing, ask the children why they feel uncomfortable about sharing in this class. Explain that sometimes everyone feels this way.

Questions and Answers

Take each question, no matter how silly or serious, and answer as best as you can.

Developing the Session

Review

Review child abuse from Session 2. What are the different kinds? Tell the children that today's session will be about a special kind of child abuse: sexual abuse.

Sexual Abuse: A Special Kind of Child Abuse

The adult leader should lead a discussion about sexual abuse. Write the children's definitions and examples on newsprint or a chalkboard.

What is sexual abuse? A formal definition might include: sexual activity between an adult or older child with a younger child which may or may not involve touching. Explain that sexual activity is kissing on the mouth and touching private parts. It is also watching movies that show people touching private parts.

List examples of sexual abuse; for example, when an adult or an older child:

Touches a child's private parts.
Takes pictures of children's private parts.
Asks a child to touch an adult's or older child's private parts.

BACKGROUND FOR THE LEADER

It is important for people to understand why it is wrong for children to be exploited by adults. Sexual contact between an adult and a child is wrong because the child is not developmentally capable of understanding the sexual activity. In addition, the child may not be able to resist the contact. Finally, the child may be psychologically and socially dependent upon the offender. Because of these factors, sexual contact between an adult and a child or an older child and a younger child is sexual exploitation.

Each teacher should review "Reporting Child Abuse: An Ethical Mandate for Ministry" in Appendix F.

God as a Shepherd/Mother Hen

Tell the parable about the lost sheep in Matthew 18:10–14. Also tell the children about the image of God as a mother hen and discuss the scripture.

- How is God described in this scripture?
- Why would the shepherd be upset about losing one sheep?
- How does God feel about the lost sheep?

- Can you think of a time when you felt lost and God helped you?
- Emphasize that God wants everyone to be safe.

Learn Ways to Protect Yourself

Tell the class that today they will be learning more about how they can help protect themselves. Ask the children what warnings they have learned from their parents and teachers in order to protect themselves from people who might hurt them. List all the ways they can think of on a chalkboard or newsprint. Examples might include:

Don't get in a car with a stranger.
Don't walk or play alone in parks.

Discuss how effective the children think these precautions are.

Do these rules work well in a situation where the grown-up is a stranger?
How effective are these rules if the grown-up who hurts children is someone the child knows?

Tell the children that most child abuse takes place between a child and a grown-up that the child knows. This course will help the children learn ways to protect themselves from grown-ups who hurt children, even when the grown-up is someone they know.
What are some clues that a child might be in danger?

Someone wants a "special" relationship to be a secret.
A child feels uncomfortable.
Our feelings tell us that something is wrong.

Remind the children that they will learn more about this in a future session.

NOTE TO THE TEACHER

Throughout these sessions, remember that children have the potential to be abusers themselves. Sometimes the experience of being abused or other trauma affects children in such a way that they use power over a younger child to build up their own self-esteem. It is therefore important that the teacher not only discuss saying "No!" to a potentially abusive situation, but also that it is the responsibility of all human beings to take care of those who are smaller and younger. It is normal for children to explore their sexuality and have sexual interest in other children who are peers or children whose age and physical size is similar. Sexual abuse involves one child or adult who is older or more powerful forcing or tricking someone younger, smaller, or less powerful to participate in sexual activity.

Activity: "What If" Game[1]

Brainstorm about possible responses that children could use when confronted by a potentially dangerous situation. Write responses on newsprint or a chalkboard.

Procedure

1. A teacher gives the class open ended "What if someone . . ." statements. The class gives possible responses. Some what if's include:

What if someone followed you home from school?
What if someone ran faster than you?
What if someone made you promise not to tell?
What if someone said that he or she would kill your dog?
What if someone invited you into his or her house, would you do it?
What if someone asked you to take your clothes off?
What if someone said your mom said it was okay?
What if someone said he or she would give you a present?
What if someone said that he or she would give you money, if you let the person touch you?

The object is to explore realistic alternatives to possible situations. This probably prohibits the use of machine guns, karate, and other unrealistic tactics.

Emphasize that if a child can't find a way out, it is still not his or her fault. It may be that the wisest response to an extremely dangerous situation is to do nothing until the child is safe and can tell someone.

NOTE TO THE TEACHER

Most of the media attention in the last few years has focused on prevention of kidnapping and sexual abuse by strangers. This could be characterized as "stranger danger." However, statistics show that most children are abused by someone they already know. According to the California Commission on the Status of Women, 80 percent of all cases of child abuse involve the assault of a child by someone she or he knows—a relative, stepparent, family friend, parent, or trusted individual.

Therefore, it is important that discussions of how to prevent sexual abuse always emphasize the difficulty of saying "no" to a trusted individual, someone the child cares about. It is much easier for discussions to focus on stranger danger, but prevention can only take place when we face the reality of abuse within our families and among our acquaintances.

Art Activity

Hand out Activity Sheet 6 and ask the children to paint a picture of a loving, supportive God. Encourage children to draw male and female images as well inanimate objects. (God is like mother, like a rainbow, like a shepherd, etc.) This will make a wonderful illustration to the prayer to be used in the conclusion. Keep these papers for sharing in the next session.

Concluding the Session

Summarize and Evaluate

Ask the children to share some ideas learned and feelings about what happened in the session.

Remind the children that the teachers are available after each session to talk. Once again, give the children a home phone number where they may reach the teacher during the week.

Tell the children about future sessions.

Closing

Ask the children either to stand or sit in a circle and to pray together the reflective prayer on Activity Sheet 6.

Sing "Shout for God" from Session 1.

Activity Sheet 6

Prayer

O God, who is like a shepherd, we thank you for the ways that you care for each of us. We pray for those children who are abused. Please comfort and care for them. Amen.

Draw a picture of a loving and supportive God.

For You to Take Home

In today's session we learned:

- God is a source of comfort.
- Some children experience child sexual abuse.
- God wants children to be safe.

Here's an activity that I can do at home.

Maze

Jesus told the story of the shepherd who lost a sheep. He hunted everywhere to find that one lost sheep. In this maze, help the shepherd find the lost sheep.

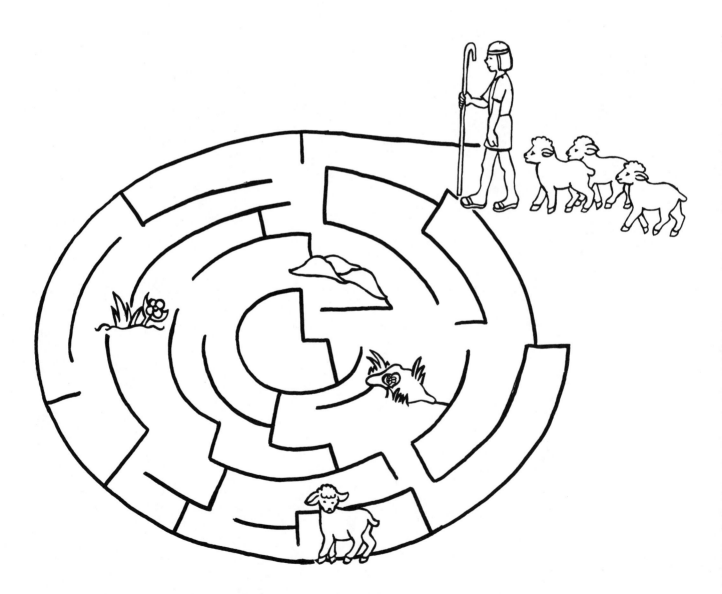

Session 5

God's Gift of Feelings

Objectives

- To increase the children's understanding that feelings are part of God's creation.
- To increase the children's awareness that feelings are a resource for response to he world.
- To be able to name and describe one's feelings.
- To increase the children's understanding that feelings can help us know how to react in certain ways.

Theological and Biblical Concepts

Through the psalms, the people of God expressed a range of emotions—anger, sadness, and happiness. They had the same feelings as we do, and they brought these feelings to God.

Like the people of God in the psalms, we too feel a range of emotions. In some situations, we feel happy and joyful; in others, anger and rage. It is important that children understand that feelings are also part of God's creation. Feelings are good and are clues to help us understand our situation. Feelings can warn us when we are in danger.

Resources Needed

Bibles
Markers and crayons
Copies of Activity Sheet 7 and the "For You to Take Home" sheet
Wall chart listing feelings
Drawings or photographs of faces that depict the feelings on the wall chart

Teacher Preparation

1. Read Psalms 6:2–3, 23:4a, 31:10, and 84:1–2. Write out these scripture passages to present to the class.

2. Make a large chart listing feelings: sad, happy, anxious, worried, frightened, angry, upset, excited, glad, etc. Also draw or cut out pictures or drawings of faces to match each feeling.
3. Review the entire lesson.
4. Make copies of Activity Sheet 7 and the "For You to Take Home" sheet.

This Session in Brief

Getting Started

Build Community (10 min)
Questions and Answers

Developing the Session

Psalms and Feelings (10 min)
Trust Your Feelings (15 min)
Activity: Chart of Feelings (15 min)

Concluding the Session (10 min)

Summarize and Evaluate
Closing

The Session Plan

Getting Started

Build Community

Ask each child to share the picture that he or she drew of a loving supportive God last session.

Questions and Answers

Ask the children if they have any questions. You may not know the answers, but assure the children that you will do your best to get answers. For the questions that you can answer, be sure that your information is accurate.

Developing the Session

Psalms and Feelings

Present the following scriptures on newsprint or poster board.

Psalm 6:2–3

> *Be gracious to me, O God, for I*
> > *am languishing;*
> *O God, heal me, for my bones*
> > *are shaking with terror.*
> *My soul also is struck with*
> > *terror,*
> *While you, O God—how long?*

Psalm 23:4a

> *Even though I walk through the*
> > *darkest valley,*
> *I fear no evil;*
> > *for you are with me.*

Psalm 31:10

> *For my life is spent with sorrow,*
> > *and my years with sighing;*
> *my strength fails because of my misery,*
> > *and my bones waste away.*

Psalm 84:1–2

> *How lovely is your dwelling place,*
> > *O God of hosts!*
> *My soul longs, indeed it faints*
> > *for the courts of the Sovereign;*
> *my heart and my flesh sing for joy*
> > *to the living God.*

Read the scriptures to the class, then each scripture.

- Do you understand the words? For example: in Psalm 6, "gracious," "languish-ing"; in Psalm 31, "waste away"; in Psalm 84, "dwelling place," "faints," "the courts of the Sovereign."
- How does speaker feel in each situation? For example: in Psalm 6, scared; in Psalm 23, comforted; in Psalm 31, sad; in Psalm 84, happy.
- Have you ever felt like that?

Trust Your Feelings

Explain to the children that God has given each person feelings. For example, when a pet is sick, we feel sad; at a birthday party, most of us are really happy.

Activity: Chart of Feelings

- Read the chart of the feelings that you prepared earlier.
- Hand out the drawings or photographs of faces to the children.
- Discuss each feeling and have the class match a drawing or photograph with the feeling.
- Ask if there are any feelings that should be added to the list?
- Ask the children if there have been times when they have had these feelings.

NOTE TO THE TEACHER

Younger elementary children love to talk about experiences that they have had. You may have to set a limit of one example for each feeling.

Also remember that different children may feel very different in the same situation. Always remember that all feelings should be validated. There are no correct answers. For example, some members may find darkness comforting and quiet, whereas others find it frightening.

Remind the children of what they learned in the last session about helping children protect themselves. Emphasize again. [It might be helpful to print the following sentences on a newsprint and hang them on the wall.]

- It is not okay for an adult or older child to touch a child's private parts except for health and safety reasons.
- It is not okay for an adult or older child to ask a child to touch his or her private parts.

Explain that feelings sometimes tell us what to do. For example:

- When the sky gets very cloudy and dark, we probably would feel a little scared and find a safe place out of the weather.
- If a little puppy was trapped in box or bucket, we would probably feel sorry for the puppy and get help.
- If an electrical wire is on the sidewalk, we would think about danger and get help.
- When a big kid who has been a bully before comes walking toward us, we would worry and go another way.
- When our pet seems to be hurt, we would be concerned and get an adult to look at the animal.
- When there is smoke in the house, we would feel scared and run out of the house to call the fire department.

Ask the children for other examples of situations when they might experience feelings that would tell them what to do.

NOTE TO THE TEACHER

Often the sexual abuse of children begins with a gradual "courting" process that the abuser uses to gain the trust of the child. The abuser may talk about caring for the child, give the child gifts, and do activities that make the child feel comfortable and safe. These actions and words confuse the child because they are similar to the actions and words of a trusted adult. Perhaps this is the most difficult part of teaching child abuse prevention, in that we must help our children understand that even actions and words that seem loving may not be. Remind the children that when they feel uncomfortable or unsafe, even in a relationship with an adult who has seemed safe, it is important to say "no" and get help.

Hand out the copies of the Activity Sheet 7 and ask the children to identify the feelings that go with each picture.

Concluding the Session

Summarize and Evaluate

Provide time for the children to talk about what they have discovered in this session.

Closing

Ask the children to stand in a circle and think of hand motions to represent different feelings. For example: shake fist, angry; raise hands high, joy; cover face with hands, sadness.

Then, while you read the psalms from the lesson, ask the class to pantomime the feelings. Each child can act out the feelings individually.

Remind the children that the teachers are available after each session to talk. Once again, give the children a home phone number where they may reach the teacher during the week.

Close class with a short prayer.

Activity Sheet 7

Feelings are clues to help us. Match the feelings to the pictures. (The names of the feelings should be written down. The children can draw a line to match the pictures.)

happy

angry

frightened

proud

sad

For You to Take Home

In today's session we learned:

- We can name and describe our feelings.
- Feelings are part of God's creation.
- Feelings help us to know what to do.

Here's an activity that we can do at home.

Hidden Message

To find a list of feelings, circle every third letter (left to right) in the puzzle. Write the letters on the lines below and divide them into words.

R	A	S	T	T	A	O	O	D	B
A	H	R	L	A	A	B	P	B	D
P	F	N	Y	I	S	F	T	F	R
C	R	I	E	D	G	T	E	H	H
W	T	D	T	E	N	W	N	D	V
E	M	N	D	I	S	W	M	R	O
D	I	R	N	E	R	H	O	I	F
N	E	G	L	D	A	P	A	L	R
N	D	G	G	B	C	R	C	D	Y

_____

_____

_____

_____

Can you think of other feelings?_____

_____

_____

_____

Hidden Message Answer: Sad, Happy, Frightened, Worried, Angry

Session 6

Good Touch/Bad Touch/ Confusing Touch

Objectives

- To help the children recognize that God intends for us to have touch that is nurturing and affirming.
- To increase the children's knowledge about good/safe, bad/unsafe, and confusing touch.

Theological and Biblical Concepts

In Matthew 19:13–15 children were brought to Jesus so that he would lay his hands on them with prayer. The disciples were going to send them away, but Jesus said, "Let the children come to me, and do not hinder them; for to such belongs the Realm of Heaven." Then Jesus touched the children.

This session explains the concepts of good/safe, bad/unsafe, and confusing touch. The Bible tells us that the touch of Jesus brought blessing and wholeness. Good touch is life giving and affirming. It is healthy and part of the life that Jesus promises us.

It is important to remember that good touch is not a luxury; it is essential for life. New babies must be held and touched in order to survive. Children do not thrive without the touch of others. Throughout the Gospels Jesus touched people. He put his hands on people in a way that blessed and comforted. Jesus' touch was life-giving. In this session, the comforting and affirming aspects of good touch should be emphasized.

Resources Needed

Newsprint and markers or chalkboard and chalk
Touching Safety Poster from Session 2
Magazines
Glue
Scissors
Large piece of cardboard (approximately 36 by 11 inches)
3- by 5-inch cards
Copies of Activity Sheets 8, 9, and 10
Copies of "For You to Take Home" page
Story: "Talking Helps" from *No More Secrets for Me* by Oralee Wachter
    (Boston: Little, Brown, 1983)

Teacher Preparation

1. Read Matthew 19:13–15. Learn the story so that you can tell it with enthusiasm and meaning. This does not mean that you must memorize the story, and you certainly may use notes. If you don't have time to learn the story, practice reading it so that you can keep the children's interest as you read. (See the note in the Introduction about storytelling.)
2. Review the entire lesson. Learn the song.
3. Make copies of Activity Sheets 8, 9, and 10 and "For You to Take Home" page.
4. Add to the "Touching Safety Rules" poster the statement: Anytime you feel mixed up about a touch . . . Tell the person to "STOP." TALK about it with a grown-up you can trust.

This Session in Brief

Getting Started (5 min)

Build Community
Questions and Answers

Developing the Session

Option 1: Talk about Touching Safety
Option 2: Touch Continuum (10 min)
Completing Sentences (5 min)
Bible Study (10 min)
Discuss Touching Safety Rules (10 min)
Group Activity (10 min)
Optional Activities

Concluding the Session (10 min)

Summarize and Evaluate
Closing

Background for the Leader

Both children and adults experience various reactions to touch from another person. We "know" the difference between a touch that makes us feel safe and affirmed and one that makes us feel uncomfortable or scared. But we rarely step back and name these feelings, much less exercise our option to say "no" when we don't like the way we are being touched.

The "Touch Continuum" is a tool to help us name our feelings about being touched. It was first developed by Cordelia Anderson in 1979 in Minneapolis. The Touch Continuum can help children learn the concept of naming their feelings and reaction to a touch and acting to set their own limits and is not simply a list of rules and regulations. However, teaching this concept to very young children may be challenging, so some guidelines can help in the beginning.

Touch can be understood in three categories:

GOOD/SAFE TOUCH: This touch is nurturing, affirming, supportive. It makes the person receiving it feel good, loved, and affirmed. It never diminishes the recipient; it does not take from the recipient. All persons need to receive this kind of touch.

CONFUSING TOUCH: This touch makes the recipient feel uncomfortable, mixed up, or funny. The intent of the toucher may not be clear. The touch may be unfamiliar. For example, when a child is asked by a parent to kiss Grandma goodbye and the child is in no mood to kiss Grandma, then she or he will feel confusion and internal conflict. Confusing touch is usually not scary, but it still may not be wanted by a child. Also confusing for a child is a medical procedure—for example, receiving an injection, which is painful but "good" because it helps make the child healthy. Perhaps the most confusing touch for a child to sort out is the touch that "feels good" but is also scary, such as a touch that is sexually stimulating but initiated by an older child who tells the child not to tell anyone. Thus touch that "feels good" is not necessarily good/safe touch.

BAD/UNSAFE TOUCH: This touch is hurtful, scary, and exploitative. It usually involves physical force or pain. It is usually very clear that the recipient does not want this kind of touch. Hitting, beating, and rape are examples of bad/unsafe touch.

The nature of touch is NOT determined:

- By the touch itself—kissing may be good/safe, confusing, or bad/unsafe.
- The good intentions of the toucher—"I was just trying to be affectionate; I didn't mean any harm."
- By who the toucher is—not all touches by a parent are necessarily good/safe; not all touches by a stranger are necessarily bad/unsafe.

The recipient of the touch ultimately decides whether the touch is good/safe, confusing, or bad/unsafe. It is the recipient who has the right to accept or not accept any particular touch from another person.

This concept of choice is the most important lesson we can teach children about touching and being touched. However, it is difficult to teach this notion of choice to young children. This is why giving young children guidelines for safe touching can be the first step in their learning process.

The following guidelines appear in *Talking about Touching for Parents and Kids—Parent Guide*, by Kathy Beland (Seattle: Committee for Children, 1988):

1. It is NEVER OKAY for grown-ups or older kids to touch your PRIVATE BODY PARTS—except to keep you healthy and clean.
2. If someone touches your private body parts and asks you to keep it a SECRET, TELL someone about it right away. If the first person doesn't believe you, tell SOMEONE ELSE!
3. Anytime you feel mixed up about a touch . . . Tell the person to "STOP." TALK about it with a grown-up you can trust.

As children practice these guidelines (see *Talking about Touching* for suggested approaches to this for children and parents), they can begin to understand the concept of the Touch Continuum.

Always be aware that there are cultural factors involved in any discussion of touching. Our understandings of appropriate and inappropriate touching are shaped by our particular cultural context. For example, in Western culture, it is common practice to greet someone with a handshake. We teach this custom to our children as a part of etiquette. In some Asian cultures, it is inappropriate to touch at all; instead the greeting is a bow from the waist. In Maori culture in New Zealand, the head of a child is considered sacred; thus adults do not touch children on the top of the head, and for a non-Maori to touch a child's head is considered an insult.

These cultural differences are yet another reason that we cannot simply teach children a list of touches that are good/safe or bad/unsafe. The particular touches will vary from culture to culture. But we can teach children that they can choose and that when they are scared or confused, they can come to us for help.

The Right and Wrong of Touching[1]

What is wrong about "bad" touch? "Bad" touch makes a person feel bad about him- or herself. A person may feel frightened, powerless, putdown, and exploited because someone they see as more powerful touches in a particular way or forces her or him to do something the person doesn't want to do. It is wrong to touch someone this way because it takes away that person's right to decide what he or she wants and makes the person feel bad. It's not wrong just because it is sexual; it's wrong because it takes advantage of the other person.

What is right about "good" touch? "Good" touch makes a person feel good about her- or himself. When someone touches another person in a positive and nonexploitative way, the person feels affirmed, accepted, respected, supported, and loved. It is touch that both people freely choose. It is right to touch someone in this way because it affirms the worth of that person as one created in God's image and therefore worthy of acceptance.

Is "good" touch always the right thing to do? It is important to understand that a "good" touch is different from touches that just feel good. People may choose to be touched or to touch another in different ways at different stages in their lives. Under some circumstances some touch is appropriate while other touch is not. What may be "good" touch in one relationship wouldn't be in another (a hug from a friend may be "good," but that same hug may be "bad" or uncomfortable from a stranger). What may be "good" touch at one point in a relationship may be "confusing" or "bad" touch at a later point (e.g., a kiss on a cheek from a relative can be "bad" or "confusing" when a person becomes a preteen). "Good" touch (by definition) is never wrong. However, it may not always be the wisest or most appropriate action.

So, is "confusing" touch right or wrong? It is confusing because it is not really clear what is going on or why someone is touching you in this way. If the person being touched feels in any way uncomfortable, frightened, or hesitant and really doesn't want to feel these things, then it is wrong to touch them this way.

Sometimes the confusion occurs because a family member touches another family member. Sometimes touches that felt "good" when a person was a small child feel uncomfortable or frightening as a person grows older.

Every person has the right not to be touched in "bad" or "confusing" ways. What are some of the responsibilities of touching? In order to respect the rights of others, it is important never to force others to be touched in a way that is "confusing" or "bad" for them.

The Session Plan

Getting Stared

Build Community

Review the following key phrases from Session 3: child abuse, physical abuse, emotional and verbal abuse, sexual abuse, offender, victim, survivor. Review Session 3 with the group.

Questions and Answers

Invite questions from the children and do your best to answer them. If you don't know the answer, tell the children you will find out.

NOTE TO THE TEACHER

As a leader, you will often get inappropriate responses from the children. Most of these responses are given because the children are uncomfortable or embarrassed by the topic. Sometimes a child might respond with a silly or "off the wall" answer because the topic is difficult to discuss, perhaps because they know someone who is being abused or because the child might be experiencing abuse. Don't let inappropriate responses get you off track; try to keep working on the topic. If responses really get out of hand, discuss with the children why a person might want to give a silly answer and suggest possible ways for the children to help people give real answers.

Developing the Session

Option 1: Talk about Touching Safety[2]

This discussion is more suited to younger children. Some suggested questions include:

- You get touches from lots of people; can you name a few? (Answers may include: Mommy, Daddy, Grandma, Grandpa, babysitters, friends.)

Explain that some touches are SAFE—when they are done with LOVE and CARE.

- Name some safe touches. (For example: head pat, hugs, taking out splinters.)

Explain that taking out a splinter is a safe touch even though it hurts sometimes.

Explain that some touches are UNSAFE.

- Name some unsafe touches (e.g., hitting, biting, hair pulling).
- Explain that these touches are not done with love and care. They are NOT OKAY.
- Ask if someone can tell about a time when someone got an unsafe touch.

Option 2: Touch Continuum

This approach is recommended for older children. First, define the following terms:

- Good/Safe Touch: warm and caring touch; makes a person feel good about her- or himself.
- Bad/Unsafe Touch: hurtful; makes a person feel bad about her- or himself.
- Confusing Touch: makes a person feel uncomfortable, uneasy, confused, unsure about the intentions of the toucher.

Explain briefly the concept of "continuum" (gradations between extremes—e.g., hot, warm, cool, cold). Then describe the "Touch Continuum" (see "Teacher Preparation").

Draw a long horizontal line on newsprint or a chalkboard to represent a continuum, label one end "good/safe" and the other, "bad/unsafe." Write "confusing" in the center. Put happy face and sad face on the line for younger nonreaders. Take the pictures of touch collected from magazines and other sources and ask the children to place them on the continuum. Ask them to recall childhood experiences of touching.

62

(For visual reinforcement, use red markers for bad/unsafe touch, green for good/safe, and brown for confusing.) Place these on the continuum. For example:

GOOD/SAFE ———— **CONFUSING** ———— **BAD/UNSAFE**

Playing patty cake. Holding hands with a friend

Uncle Joe's mushy kiss. An overpowering hug from a family friend.

Spanking. Being punched by a brother or sister A shot from doctor

---

NOTE TO THE TEACHER

Using the "Touch Continuum" helps participants to identify and categorize their own experience as well as to affirm their feelings about those experiences. It gives them permission to feel good, bad, or confused about being touched.

Completing Sentences

Ask the children to finish the sentences about touching:

I feel bad when . . . .
I feel good when . . . .
I feel confused when . . . .

Here are some sample answers. Ask the children to identify the "someone" by role—not by name—and describe the touch. For example:

I feel bad when I am spanked.
I feel good when a friend gives me a hug.
I feel confused when someone I don't know very well puts his arm around me.

Try to elicit responses for each category. Be sure to use examples of confusing and bad touch in the family or with girlfriends or boyfriends. Write some examples on the continuum line that you drew.

Bible Study

Tell the story of Jesus and the children in Matthew 19:13–15 and discuss the text. (See the "Theological and Biblical Concepts.")

- What kind of touch was Jesus' touch?
- Why did the disciples want the children to go away?
- Why do you think that Jesus thought it was important to talk to the children and bless them?
- How do you think the children felt when the disciples told them to go away?
- How do you think the children felt when Jesus invited them to come to him?
- Can you think of why touching is so important to babies?

Discuss Touching Safety Rules

- Review the personal rights discussed in Session 1 by asking the children to name a few.
- Review Touching Safety Rules from Session 2.
- Explain the rule that was added in this session.
- Emphasize that anytime a touch is confusing, it is important to talk to a grown-up or someone who is trusted.

NOTE TO THE TEACHER

Emphasize the following concepts:
- It is wrong to touch someone else in an unsafe way. It is wrong for someone to touch you if you don't want to be touched that way or at that time.
- You do not have to tolerate being touched in any way that makes you feel bad/unsafe or confused. You can and should decide who touches you and how they can touch you.
- Remember, "no" means no and "yes" means yes. Don't get into the "if she or he says 'no' she or he means 'yes'" game. Everyone loses. Be as clear and straightforward as you can.

Group Activity

Make a collage of touching. On a long piece of cardboard, have the group glue pictures that are examples of good, bad, and confusing touch.

Optional Activities

Story: "Talking Helps" in *No More Secrets for Me* (see resources)
Activity Sheet 8, "Some Touches Don't Feel Good," and/or Activity Sheet 9, "Sometimes Hugs and Other Good Touches Can Be Confusing"

Concluding the Session

Summarize and Evaluate

Encourage the children to think about what they learned in this session. What new things did they learn? What things did they already know about?

Remind the children that the teachers are available after each session to talk. Once again give the children a home phone number where they may reach the teacher during the week.

Closing

Introduce the song on Activity Sheet 10 and discuss the ideas in the song with the children.

Activity Sheet 8

Some Touches Don't Feel Good

Draw a picture that shows when someone touched you in a way you did not like.

Activity Sheet 9

Sometimes Hugs and Other Good Touches Can Be Confusing[3]

Good touches can sometimes feel bad or confusing when:

- We are not expecting them.
- The touch is from a stranger or someone we don't know well.
- The touch becomes uncomfortable.
- We feel embarrassed by the touch.

How do you think the children in these pictures felt about these touches?

Activity Sheet 10

God Made Flowers

Words by
Walter Farquharson

Music by
Ron Klusmeier

Note: The keyboard introduction as it appears represents one option; another is to play measures 3–4 and 17–18, as marked.

Introduction

(Alternate introduction)   (to m. 17)

God made flow - ers,   God made trees,   cat - er - pil - lars,   and bum - ble - bees.
God made chil - dren,   grown - ups, too,   gave us all some   work to do.

God made el - bows,   God made knees,   pol - lens and dusts that   make us sneeze.
Help us, God, to   love you more,   keep good friends and   find some more.

Help us, God,   to love and care,   laughs and tick - les   and hugs to share.

Help us, God, to love and care, laughs and tick-les and hugs to share.

Words by Walter Farquharson, music by Ron Klusmeier. Cascade, Wisc.: Worship Arts—Resources for Ministry, 1986, *Just Like Salt*, p. 66.

For You to Take Home

In today's session we learned:

- God intends for us to have touch that is nurturing and affirming.
- Some touches are bad or confusing because they make me feel bad or uncomfortable.

Here's an activity that I can do at home:

Touches I Like

Many touches are very good. They make you feel good about yourself and help you feel great. Circle the touches that are enjoyable. Draw a picture of a good touch in the blank place.

Session 7

God Gives Us Courage

Objectives

- To help children learn that God empowers us and gives us strength against tremendous odds.
- To practice ways children can respond to abusive behavior.
- To practice ways children can try to stop ongoing abuse in their lives or in the lives of their friends.

Theological and Biblical Concepts

The Hebrew Scriptures story of Miriam, Moses' sister (Exodus 2:1–10), tells of a young girl's bravery and courage. Although Moses' sister is not named in this particular text, the biblical genealogies name Miriam as Moses' only sister (Numbers 26:59 and 1 Chronicles 6:3). Later biblical texts tell us that she grew up to be a leader of the Hebrew people during the exodus from Egypt.

The text in Exodus 2 tells about the pharaoh's decree that all Hebrew boys be killed. Young Miriam lives with her family in captivity in Egypt where her people suffer greatly. In this setting, this young Hebrew girl has the courage to speak out. Baby Moses is put in a basket in the river to hide him from Pharaoh. Miriam is assigned by her mother to watch over him. When the Pharaoh's daughter discovers the baby, it is Miriam who suggests that she should hire a Hebrew nurse to care for the baby. Miriam protects her baby brother from harm. Even though she is young, she is brave. This bravery is what will help her someday be a leader of her people.

Everyone needs to be reminded about the courage and bravery that are needed when people are oppressed and afraid. Miriam shows what positive action can do. She reminds us all that no matter what our age, we cam take action to make situations better. God helped Miriam be strong and brave.

Resources Needed

Newsprint and markers, or chalkboard and chalk
Copies of the "For You to Take Home" page
Story: "What If," in *No More Secrets for Me*, by Oralee Wachter
    (Boston: Little, Brown, 1983)
Puppets from Session 3

Teacher Preparation

1. Read Exodus 2:1–10. Learn the story so that you can tell it with enthusiasm and meaning. This does not mean that you must memorize it and you certainly may use notes. If you don't have time to learn the story, practice reading it so that you can keep the children's interest as you read. (See the note in the Introduction about storytelling.)
2. Review the entire lesson.
3. Prepare for the puppet play. Either use a real puppet stage or make a puppet stage with some sheets and a table.
4. Make copies of the "For You to Take Home" page.

This Session in Brief

Getting Started (10 min)

Build Community
Questions and Answers

Developing the Session (40 min)

The Story of Miriam
Teaching Prevention Rules
Puppet Play
Ways That Children Are Tricked
Optional Activities

Concluding the Session (10 min)

Summarize and Evaluate
Closing

The Session Plan

Getting Started

Build Community

Describe briefly the plan for the session today. Take a few minutes to ask each child what they remember from the previous sessions.

Questions and Answers

Answer any questions that the children have.

Developing the Session

The Story of Miriam

Tell the story in Exodus 2:1–10. Then discuss the story:

- What happens in this story?
- How does this story of a young girl's bravery make you feel?
- Why do you think Miriam had the courage to speak to the Pharaoh's daughter?

Teaching Prevention Rules

Have the children make a *new* list of how to protect themselves. Write this list on newsprint or chalkboard. Be sure that the following items are emphasized:

- Trust your feelings.
- Stay away from someone when you think that person might hurt you.
- Say "No!" (This does not always work, but try it anyway.)
- Tell a trusted adult.

Puppet Play

Use the puppets from Session 3 or, if time permits, new puppets can be made. Sock puppets, paper bag puppets, or shadow puppets can be used for these activities.

NOTE TO THE TEACHER

Shadow puppets can be made by children by cutting animal or people shapes out of cardboard. Tape the figure to a stick or pencil so it can be held up. Next, put up a sheet as a screen. Have children stand behind the sheet with a light behind them. They can kneel behind a table and hold up puppets to cast a shadow on the screen for the class to watch.[1]

Here is a story to narrate for the puppet play.

> *Kesha and Martin are twin brother and sister. They have one older sister. Their parents work every day, so after school Kesha and Martin go to an after-school program. One day a man who worked as a volunteer teacher for the program invited them to go to another room for a special reading time. After the teacher read a story to them, he asked them if they liked boys and girls.*

Kesha and Martin didn't know what to tell the grown-up. Their friends at school were both boys and girls. The teacher asked them if they had ever seen a man without any clothes on. The teacher then showed them some pictures of naked people. After that the teacher took off his clothes.

When the kids were finally allowed to go to back to play with the other children, they both felt really embarrassed and confused. Kesha and Martin talked about what happened and decided to talk to their older sister. Maybe she could tell them what to do.

Ask three children to use the puppets to take the parts of Kesha, Martin, and their older sister Susan. (If there are children in your class with those names, be sure to substitute other names.) Tell "Susan" that she is to be helpful as she can. Ask the group to think about what they would say in Susan's place.

After the trio has tried some dialogue, ask the class for other suggestions about what would help the children and what may make things worse. (Helpful—believe them, be serious, help them to tell a trusted adult. Unhelpful—laugh, tell everyone else at school, be really embarrassed.)

Brainstorm about what to do if Susan had not been helpful. What should the twins do next? Who else could they talk to?

NOTE TO THE TEACHER

Puppets can be a terrific way to practice skills learned in these sessions. This particular puppet activity's objective is to practice and increase awareness of peer support of person victimized by sexual assault.

Successful puppet play depends of many different things. Pay special attention to the following points.

- Make the atmosphere relaxed.
- Use as many children as possible—let them all have a chance to answer questions and operate the puppets.
- **Use only volunteers, never ask a child to participate.**
- Use leaders to fill extra roles if needed.
- Even when using puppets, never ask a child to play a victim. Begin the puppet play by having the children act out what can be done to stop the abuse from happening. Have the puppets discuss who they can trust, how to get away, and how to get help. This puppet play should be an empowering experience in which the child learns about possible options to prevent or stop the abuse.

If the children have never used puppets before, use a simpler situation or a demonstration first. Then ask the children to do a more complicated situation.

For more puppet plays, see Carol A. Plummer, *Preventing Sexual Abuse* (Holmes Beach, Fla.: Learning Publications, 1984), pp. 68–74.

Ways That Children Are Tricked

Ask the children what ideas they have about how a grown-up or older child might try to trick a child. List examples of each.

> **Bribe:** "I'll give you some money for video games." "I'll buy you a new bike." "I'll let you pet my new puppies."
>
> **Threats:** "I'll tell everyone that you did it anyway." "I'll kill your dog." "Something just might happen to your parents." "I won't let you play with your friends ever again."
>
> **Confuse:** "It will feel good, don't be scared." "Everyone does things like this." "We'll make it our little secret." "You are bad and deserve to be punished." "I need you to do this for me." "Your parent was hit by a car. Come with me to the hospital."

Take the list of rules that the children suggested at the beginning of this session, review it, and add any additional ideas that the children have after the puppet play.

Optional Activities

Read the story "What If," in *No More Secrets for Me*, by Oralee Wachter (Boston: Little, Brown, 1983). Ask the children:

- What kind of abuse takes place in this situation.
- How do the children help one another?
- What made these four children such good friends?
- How could each person be helped by a friend?
- Is there anything else he or she could have done?
- How could the church help these children?

Concluding the Session

Summarize and Evaluate

Spend a few minutes recalling what has happened during the session. Answer any questions about this session and give the children some ideas about what will happen in future sessions.

Remind the children that the teachers are available after each session to talk. Once again give the children a home phone number where they may reach the teacher during the week.

Closing

Ask the children to stand or sit in a circle and to pray together the reflective prayer on the "For You to Take Home" page.

Sing your choice of a new song learned during this course.

For You to Take Home

In today's session we learned:

- God gives us strength against tremendous odds.
- We can learn ways to respond to abuse.

Here's an activity that we can do at home.

Dot-to-Dot

Miriam bravely suggested that the Pharaoh's daughter get a Hebrew nurse for the baby Moses. The Hebrew nurse was really the baby's mother. Connect the dots to see the picture.

O God, we thank you for ways to help make changes in our lives. We know that changing situations is not easy. We pray for courage and strength to make changes. Help us to be brave and strong like Miriam. Amen.

Session 8

No More Secrets

Objectives

- To increase participants' awareness that we experience the love of God through the help and presence of others.
- To explore ways to tell a trusted adult about abuse.
- To explore ways to help a friend who has experienced sexual assault.

Theological and Biblical Concepts

In Luke 10:25–37 Jesus answers a question from a lawyer about eternal life by telling the parable of the Good Samaritan. This parable, or example story, begins on the road from Jerusalem to Jericho where a traveler is beaten by robbers and left for dead along the roadside. The behavior of both the priest and the Levite (a Temple assistant) is in sharp contrast to the help and aid given by a foreigner, a Samaritan. The Samaritan is caring and concerned, even to the point of delaying his own journey. He uses his own money to provide a place for the traveler to heal.

From the Hebrew point of view at that time, the Samaritan is not only a foreigner, but also ceremonially unclean, a social outcast, and a religious heretic. He is the opposite of the priest, the Levite, and also the lawyer.

Jesus asks the lawyer, "Who do you think is the real neighbor?" Of course, the lawyer responded that the one who showed mercy is the neighbor, and Jesus says that the lawyer should go and do likewise.

This parable describes the caring and concern of one person who took care of someone in need. In this wonderfully direct way, Jesus charges us to become a caring community. To show our love of God, we reach out to others in need.

The people of God are a community that cares about others. This community is the church. The people of God and the church are a resource for those in need. The church may be a place where a survivor can find help. In addition, each person, as a person of God, can be a friend to others. If each person has some idea about what to do when someone comes to them for help, the person can be a better friend. Helping others expresses our love of God.

Resources Needed

Newsprint and markers or chalkboard and chalk
Wooden figures, fabric, and ribbon to tell the parable
Copies of Activity Sheets 11 and 12 and "For You to Take Home" page
Puppets and puppet theater from Sessions 3 and 7

Teacher Preparation

1. Read Luke 10:25–37. Learn the story so that you can tell it with enthusiasm and meaning. This story is especially suited to be told with small figures to illustrate the parable. Use a cloth and ribbon to make a road, some plain wooden blocks to make an inn, and some simple wooden figures to be the traveler, the priest, the Levite, the Samaritan, and the innkeeper. Don't forget the donkey to carry the traveler back to the inn. Collect your materials and practice this parable so that it can be told smoothly. (See the note in the Introduction about storytelling.)
2. Review the entire lesson. Learn the song.
3. Make copies of Activity Sheets 11 and 12 and "For You to Take Home" page.

This Session in Brief

Getting Started (10 min)

Build Community
Questions and Answers

Developing the Session (40 min)

Review Prevention
The Good Samaritan
Whom Can You Tell?
Puppet Play
Optional Activity
Help a Friend
What Happens If I Tell?
The Victim/Survivor Is Not at Fault
Optional Activity

Concluding the Session (10 min)

Summarize and Evaluate
Closing
Answers for Word Scramble Puzzle

The Session Plan

Getting Started

Build Community

Ask the children what they remember as the most important points in the last session.

Questions and Answers

Ask if anyone has any questions.

Developing the Session

Review Prevention

Briefly review the prevention rules from the last session about what to do if someone tries to hurt a child.

NOTE TO THE TEACHER

When working with younger elementary-school-age children, it is very important to give only a little information each day. Also it is essential that the teacher repeat the important points frequently. Reviewing the last session reinforces learning and also helps children who have missed a session to catch up.

Bible Study

Tell the story of the good Samaritan (Luke 10:25–37) and invite the children to discuss it.

What happened to the traveler?
Why would some people just pass by?
Why did the Samaritan stop and help?
The lawyer wanted to know who his neighbor was. Why would Jesus tell this story?
What was Jesus trying to tell us that we should do?
What would Jesus want us to do if we saw someone who had been robbed and beaten?
What would Jesus want us to do for someone who needs a different kind of help?

NOTE TO THE TEACHER

Although saying "no" is a skill that children need to prevent abuse, many molesters say that the real deterrent to them is not a child's refusal but the likelihood that a child will tell. Adult survivors of child abuse often agree. All too often the abuse itself is so threatening and brutal that saying "no" does not stop it from happening. However, a child's willingness to tell someone can be a deterrent. Advise the children that telling an abusive adult that they will tell might make a difference.

Whom Can You Tell?

On newsprint or a chalkboard, make a list of all the people that the children can think of who could be trusted to talk to about sexual abuse if it happens to them or someone they know. The children may be reluctant to use names. Therefore, people can be identified by their role or job. The list could include:

A special teacher
The school nurse
A parent
A grandparent
Church school teacher

Remind the children that each of their lists would probably be different because each of us feels close to different people and would feel more comfortable talking to special people in our lives.

Ask the children what they should do if the person that they choose to talk to doesn't believe them. Explain that sometimes grown-ups think that the child is making up the story.

Hand out Activity Sheet 11 and give the children a few minutes to complete the exercise.

NOTE TO THE TEACHER

Puppet play is an excellent way to learn and practice skills. Use the puppet play as an opportunity for the children to learn prevention skills in a safe environment. Remember:

- Introduce the activity as "pretending." This pretending is skill practice.
- Do not comment on a child's performance. Any evaluation should concern the child's use of information and skills.
- Give lots of positive reinforcement. Making puppets move and talk can be frightening. Children may need lots of encouragement.
- **Use only volunteers for puppet plays.** Never draft children. Recognize that sexual abuse may be a current concern for some of the children.

Puppet Play[1]

Use the following outline[1] to create a puppet play in which the children can learn the importance of talking with a trusted person. Begin by reading the following story.

Maria has a stepbrother named Jason. She really likes her stepbrother.
Since he is a teenager, he can drive her to the mall and the movies.
Recently Jason has been acting strange. Sometimes he stares at her.
He tells her dirty jokes and tries to rub her between her legs.

Ask the children to list people whom Maria could tell.

Then ask four children to use puppets to represent some of these people. Try to include two adult characters and two children. Assign a character to each of the children. Instruct the puppets to be helpful with Maria's problem, but explain that sometimes grown-ups don't believe children. Remind children that they must tell again and again until someone believes them.

Ask someone to play Maria and to try to tell these people about her stepbrother.

NOTE TO THE TEACHER

Often the first person that a child tells about ongoing abuse is a trusted friend of the same age. Therefore, it is essential that prevention training include teaching children what to do if a friend discloses abuse. The abused child may have no one that he or she trusts, but a friend may be influential in getting help.

NOTE TO THE TEACHER

After puppet plays, the adult leader should affirm persons and ideas. The affirmation can be either for the individual or the whole group. Some examples include: "Some good ways and ideas shared today were . . ." or "Thank you for sharing. . . ."

Optional Activity

It is a good idea in working with younger children for the teachers to participate in role playing. Have two adults act out a situation in which two children have a conversation. One child tells the other about something bad that happened to him or her; for example, one's bike is stolen or a bully takes his or her lunch money. The second adult should listen, show that he or she cares, and suggest that together they seek help from an adult. This will model what a friend can do.

Do this role play before asking the children to brainstorm about what a person can do for a friend.

Help a Friend

Review what can be done if a friend comes to talk to someone from this class:

- Listen.
- Talk.
- Show you care.
- Tell your friend to tell an adult who can help.
- Go with your friend to tell an adult.
- Give the friend suggestions about who could be trusted.
- Give the friend information about where to get help.

Ask the children how they might feel when a friend tells you about being hurt. Situations might include being abused on a trip, being a victim of advances by an older teenager, being abused by a family member. Some of the feelings might include:

- Embarrassed
- Strange
- Uncomfortable
- Nervous
- Disbelieving

Explain that very often when a child is being sexually abused, he or she doesn't really trust anyone. It might be important that someone in this class could bring the friend to someone they trust.

What Happens If I Tell?

In order to stop someone from hurting children, the crime must be reported; that is the only way that the grown-up who is hurting children can be helped.

Explain that in some cases the police need to be called; sometimes child protective services needs to be called; a doctor may be called or the child taken to a hospital to make sure he or she is okay.

Emphasize that there are many reasons why a child might be afraid. A child might worry that the family will be separated or that someone he or she cares about might go to jail. Sometimes a child has been threatened and the child thinks that the abuser will carry out those threats.

The most important thing is that the child is safe. The grown-ups will try to be as helpful as they can to stop the hurting.

NOTE TO THE TEACHER

Every church should have a list of local agencies and phone numbers for child abuse councils, child protective services, and other child service agencies. These organizations have pamphlets, cards, and lists of other resources. Every church should have a list of social agencies and referral numbers for child abuse, rape crisis, women's shelters, and other related issues. See Appendix D, "Reporting Child Abuse"; Appendix E, "What Happens When a Report Is Made"; and Appendix F, "Reporting Child Abuse: An Ethical Mandate for Ministry."

The Victim/Survivor Is Not at Fault

Finally, reinforce the idea that no matter what happens to a child, God loves each one. It is never the child's fault if something bad or hurtful happens. Sometimes a child may have broken a parental rule, such as going someplace where they shouldn't have, but this is not a reason for a child to blame him- or herself for abuse.

Explain to the children that we would like to believe that the church is a safe place, but sometimes it isn't. However, we hope that the church is a place where there are some trusted adults who care about children. The community of the church is a place where each of us can grow and heal. We can experience the love of God through the caring of people.

NOTE TO THE TEACHER

While information about whom to tell may not protect children from abuse, this kind of information can greatly reduce the duration of an abusive experience. A child who knows where to go after some experience of abuse may be able to stop it from continuing.

Optional Activity

Ask the children to make up a modern-day version of the good Samaritan story. Who would the characters be today? Where might this story happen?

Concluding the Session

Summarize and Evaluate

Ask the children for comments and questions that they might have concerning the topic of this course. Assure them that you will be available to them if they want to talk more about any of the topics in this class or just to talk. Remind the children that the teachers will be available before and after class, as well as during the week. Give them a phone number where a teacher can be reached.

Closing

Ask the children to stand or sit in a circle and to sing "Jesus Talked to Children" on Activity Sheet 12.

ANSWERS FOR SCRAMBLED WORDS ON THE "FOR YOU TO TAKE HOME" PAGE

Whom can you SRUTT?	TRUST
A hurt child needs PLEH.	HELP
People show that God EACRS.	CARES
Sometimes we feel GNYRA.	ANGRY
You are PCILASE to God.	SPECIAL
Every child needs someone to KTLA to.	TALK
God wants you to be FESA.	SAFE
NO MORE	SECRETS!

Activity Sheet 11

"Whom Can I Talk To?"

Activity Sheet 12

Jesus Talked to Children

Words by
Walter Farquharson

Music by
Ron Klusmeier

Words by Walter Farquharson, music by Ron Klusmeier, Worship Arts: Resources for Ministry, 1986, *Just Like Salt*, p. 18.

For You to Take Home

In today's session we learned:

- We experience the love of God through the help and presence of others.
- I can talk to a trusted adult about abuse.
- I know how I can help a friend who has been abused.

Here's an activity that I can do at home.

Scrambled Words

Unscramble these words from today's lesson. Print them on the right side. Then print the circled letters on the line below. They will tell you . . .

Who can you SRUTT?   __ __ _Ⓞ_ __

A hurt child needs PLEH.   _Ⓞ_ __ __

People show that God SEACR.   Ⓞ__ __ __ __

Sometimes we feel GNYRA.   __ __ _Ⓞ_ __

You are PCILASE to God.   __ _Ⓞ_ __ __ __ __

Every child needs someone to KTLA to.   Ⓞ__ __ __

God wants you to be FESA.   Ⓞ__ __ __

NO MORE __ __ __ __ __ __ __!

Session 9

Justice and Forgiveness: Responding to Harm

Objectives

- To help the children learn about forgiveness and that they are not obligated to forgive when there is no justice.
- To help the children identify and affirm their need for justice before forgiveness is possible.

Theological and Biblical Concepts

In Luke 19:1–10, Jesus visits the home of Zacchaeus, a tax collector. Zacchaeus is a sinner who has profited from taking advantage of others. After talking with Jesus, not only does he admit his guilt but he offers restitution. He will return four times the money to those from whom he has stolen. He shows that he is sorry by taking action.

This interaction between Zacchaeus and Jesus reminds us that justice and forgiveness are interrelated. Zacchaeus is a model for bringing restitution and action together with his apology. Before someone can be forgiven, he or she must repent. The words, "I am sorry. It will never, ever happen again," are crucial to forgiveness, but they are not sufficient. Action must accompany these words.

All too often, survivors of abuse and violence are told that they must forgive the offender. Even when the offender denies the violence and continues to abuse other victims, our culture, particularly Christians and churches, pressure survivors to forgive.

Resources Needed

Activity Sheet 13

Teacher Preparation

1. Read Luke 19:1–10. Learn the story so that you can tell it with enthusiasm and meaning. That does not mean that you must memorize the story, and you certainly may use notes. If you don't have time to learn the story, practice reading it so that you can keep the children's interest as you read. (See the note in the Introduction about storytelling.)
2. Have pictures ready to use in the class discussion.

This Session in Brief

Getting Started (10 min)

Build Community

Developing the Session

Bible Study (10 min)
Story and Discussion (20 min)
Additional Bible Study (15 min)

Concluding the Session (5 min)

Summarize and Evaluate
Closing

The Session Plan

Getting Started

Build Community

Show the pictures on Activity Sheet 13 and ask the children to make up story about how each hurt happened. Talk about the differences.

- How do the people feel in each picture?
- How are the injuries different?
- How are people affected?
- How do we feel when someone hurts us on purpose?
- What do we it when someone hurts us on purpose?

Developing the Session

Bible Study

Tell the story of Zacchaeus (Luke 19:1–10) and ask the children to talk about what the people from whom Zacchaeus stole might feel about him?

- What does "forgiveness" mean? ["to let go of hurt"]
- Why does Zacchaeus pay back the money?
- What does Zacchaeus plan to do so that people know that he is really sorry?

Remind the children that sometimes the anger and hurt can be so deep that it is difficult to forgive.

Ask the children, "What are the two steps that Zacchaeus took to show Jesus that he had really changed?" Write these answers on a chalkboard or newsprint:

- Zacchaeus said that he was sorry and he would not steal again.
- Zacchaeus returned four times the amount of money he had stolen.

NOTE TO THE TEACHER

After reading this story, it is essential that the teacher allow lots of time for the children to talk about their feelings. Encourage discussion to allow them to express any anxiety that the story might cause.

Story

Read the following story. Pause, where indicated, to ask the questions.

Once there was a girl named Amanda. She was five years old. She lived in a big city with her mom and her little sister, Jessica. Amanda loved to ride her bike. She liked to play with her toy kitchen and pretend to make food. She always helped her mother keep the house clean. Her mother would read her stories before bed time. She loved being with her mom.

Amanda's family went to church regularly. Her mother was on important committees at the church. At church her mother met a man who did not have any children. His name was George. Her mom started to date George. Sometimes Amanda's mom and George would take both Amanda and Jessica on trips. Amanda liked George a lot. He told great stories. Amanda was very glad when her mom said that she and George were going to get married. George would be her stepdad.

Amanda went to after-school child care. One day George came to pick up Amanda at school. Instead of taking her to her after-school program, George told Amanda that he would take her home. He said that he wanted to tell Amanda some stories and read to her until Amanda's mom came home from work.

George drove her to his house. When they got into the living room, he got out some magazines to read to Amanda. But the magazines were not for children. There were naked people in the magazines. George told her that he wanted to touch her. She didn't understand what he meant. He started to take her clothes off. He started to rub her private parts.

How do you think Amanda felt?

Amanda was scared. She knew that she did not like George touching her, but she didn't know what to do. After he told her to put her clothes on, he made her promise that she wouldn't tell anyone about this. He said that if she told, he would never let her see her mother again. She didn't tell.

What would you have done?

NOTE TO THE TEACHER

During the discussion, carefully notice responses from the children who would blame or hold Amanda responsible. For example, "She should have just run away." Follow up blaming statements with additional questions, so that participants understand that there may have been nothing Jessica could have done at that time. For example, respond by saying, "Do you think she could have run away?"

A week later, George came again to pick up Amanda after school. He did the same thing that he had done before. Again he made her feel scared.

But Amanda decided that she would go to her mother. She knew that her mother would know what to do and would protect her.

Her mother was shocked at Amanda's story, but she believed everything Amanda said. She called the Sexual Abuse Center and asked for their help. Her mother decided to talk to George. He denied everything. He said that Amanda always made up stories, that she asked him to take his pants off.

Amanda and her mother were very angry with George. Her mother called the police. They told George that he would have to talk with the police and the counselor at the Sexual Abuse Center. They made certain that Amanda was never left alone with him again. He was never allowed to pick Amanda up after school. He also had to live in his own apartment away from Amanda so that she would be safe.

How do you think Amanda felt? (Possible responses may include: grateful, embarrassed, still scared.)

Amanda told her best friend, Wendy, what had happened. Wendy was very surprised, but she also believed Amanda and stood by her. Wendy told Amanda that the Bible said she should forgive her mother's ex-boyfriend, that if she was really a good Christian she would want to forgive him and be his friend. Wendy said that would make everything fine again.

If Amanda followed Wendy's advice, do you think everything would be fine now?

How do you think Amanda felt about this talk with Wendy? (Possible responses may include: confused, upset, angry, relieved, obligated, guilty, etc.)

How do you think she felt about forgiving George at this point?

Amanda did not like to hear Wendy say this. Amanda still felt angry about what her mother's ex-boyfriend had done to her.

George had to appear in court. Amanda went to court with her mother and told her story there. Her mother reminded her that this was not her fault. George admitted what he had done, but he made it sound like it was really Amanda's fault. Even though he said he was sorry, Amanda could tell he didn't really mean it. The judge said that George was guilty of child molesting, that it was very wrong, that he should never have done these things to Amanda. Then the judge ordered George to go to counseling for three years.

Several months later, Amanda began to think about what Wendy had said about forgiveness. She still felt guilty because she hadn't forgiven George. So she went to her minister for a talk. Her minister, whose name was Ron, listened to her story. Reverend Ron told Amanda how sorry he was that all of this had happened to her. Amanda asked if she had to forgive George for what he had done. Reverend Ron said she didn't have to forgive him until she was ready. Forgiveness, he explained, is a gift that God gives us to help us heal from painful experiences. It is a way to be able to move past the painful memories and get on with our lives.

Reverend Ron reminded Amanda of the time that she and her little sister had been riding bikes. Jessica accidentally ran into Amanda. Amanda crashed and scraped her knee. It bled so much that her mother took her to the doctor to have the wound stitched up. Her sister went along and held her hand. She told her how sorry she was to have hurt her. Her sister said that she should have been more careful and that she would never play that way again.

Reverend Ron asked Amanda to look at her knee. Did she see the scar that was left from the cut? She answered "yes." Does she think about this painful event every day? "No," said Amanda; "only when I see the scar." Had she forgiven her sister for hurting her? "Yes," said Amanda. "Jessica was sorry for what she did."

"That's right," Reverend Ron said. "Your sister was sorry, and she also took responsibility for being careless. Because she did those things, you were ready to forgive her. And that has meant that you put the whole experience behind you and hardly ever think about it any more."

We need some things to happen before we are ready to forgive. We call these things "justice." We need the people around us who love us to support us when we are hurt and scared. We need our parents and other adults to help and protect us. We need the person who hurt us to take responsibility, to say that he or she is sorry, to promise never to hurt us again. "You will know when you are ready to forgive," said Reverend Ron. "When you are ready, God will help you and will put the memories of your abuse in the back of your mind so you won't think of it very often. Then you can continue to grow into a young woman who will always know that you are loved by God and by your family and friends."

How do you think Amanda feels after talking with Reverend Ron?

Ask participants to think of a time that someone their own age did something that hurt them. For example, when someone is called names, has a toy broken, or has his or her money stolen.

- How does the child who is hurt feel?
- Did the child automatically forgive the person who caused the hurt?
- Did the child ever forgive that person?

Ask participants to think of a time when someone older did something that hurt them. For example, when a grown-up breaks a promise, or hits a child, or yells.

- How does the child who is hurt feel?
- Did the child automatically forgive the person who hurt him or her?
- Did the child ever forgive that person?

Additional Bible Study

Remind the story of Zacchaeus (Luke 19:1–10) to the class.

Zacchaeus is sorry that he cheated people. He had done something wrong and he wanted to be forgiven. But he had to show everyone that he is really sorry. So Zacchaeus promises to return four times the money to people. With this action, the people knew that he really was sorry for what he had done and that he will not do it again.

Zacchaeus sinned by taking money from people, but there are many things that people can do that are wrong. Jesus was very proud of what Zacchaeus was going to do. Jesus said, "Today salvation has come to this house" (NRSV). When an adult or an older child harms children, it is important that some adults, including the police, go to that person and tell him or her that they know what has been done. They also need to tell the person who harms children to stop hurting other children. If the person who has hurt others *repents,* we should forgive him. To repent means to say that a person admits hurting someone and promises to never, ever do it again. This means making big changes.

Zacchaeus made big changes by paying back four times the amount of money he had taken. In order for people who hurt children to make big changes, they need to admit what they have done and to accept counseling and help. Only then can we forgive them.

NOTE TO THE TEACHER

Be careful not to reinforce a child's sense of obligation to forgive harm done in the absence of the abuser's repentance and justice.

Concluding the Session

Summarize and Evaluate

Ask the children to shut their eyes and think of words that were important to them today. Ask them to share words they feel comfortable sharing.

Remind the children that the teachers are available after each session to talk. Once again give the children a home phone number where they may reach the teacher during the week.

Closing

Ask the children to sit or stand in a circle. Read Psalm 119:76 aloud. "Let your constant love comfort me, as you have promised me, your servant" (*Good News Bible*).

Use the following prayer to close the session:

O God, we are reminded that you love each of us. Your constant love is with us every day. Thank you for your love and care. Amen.

Activity Sheet 13

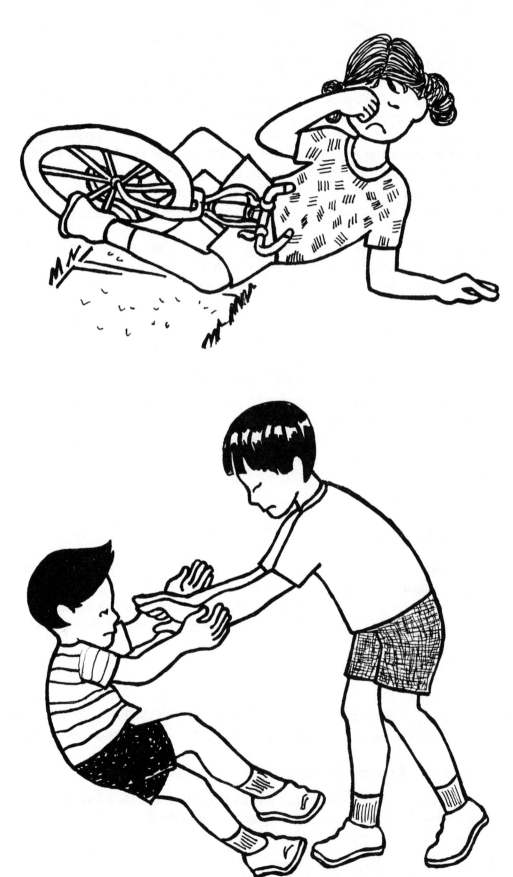

For You to Take Home

In today's session we learned

- Zacchaeus was sorry he stole money and promised Jesus he would pay everyone back.
- A person needs to say that he or she is sorry and that it will never happen again before forgiveness can happen.

Here's an activity that I can do at home.

Crossword Puzzle

See if you can put words from today's Bible story into the crossword puzzle. If you need help, use the word list.

Word List

forgiven
Zacchaeus
sorry
Jesus
money
show
tax collector

_____ (1 across) was a _____ (2 down). He told _____ (3 down) that he was _____ (4 across). He would give back four times the _____ (5 across) he had stolen. Before Zacchaeus was _____ (6 across), he had to say he was sorry and try to _____ (7 down) that he was truly sorry.

Session 10

Wrapping Up with a Positive Self-Image

Objectives

- To increase the children's understanding that God loves each child.
- To review the major concepts of the curriculum.
- To bring closure to the children's experience.

Theological and Biblical Concepts

In Romans 8:35–39, Paul reminds us of God's great love for all and tells people how much God cares about them. The translation used in this session is special because it is taken from a Native American edition of the Bible.

Paul clearly explains that Jesus' death on the cross proves the deep love that God is "for us" not "against us." This is the very heart of Paul's message to Christians. No matter what happens to us, God still loves us.

The experience of Native Americans is reflected in this translation of the scripture. Hunger, sickness, floods, wars, poverty, mistreatment, and abuse have been and are still part of many Native American peoples' lives. But for them, as well as for others of us, none of these things can keep us from God's love.

This message is important to all of us. A basic tenet of our faith is that each human being is of infinite worth. The Bible reminds us that God loves and will always be with us. When tragedy and bad things happen, God comforts us and helps us heal. The people of God are a resource to help us.

Resources Needed

Copies of "For You to Take Home" page
Yarn of various colors
Cardboard rectangle, 2 by 3 inches
String or rubber band

Teacher Preparation

1. Read Romans 8:35–39. Learn the text so that you can tell it with enthusiasm and meaning. You can use notes or write it on a big chart so the children can read along.
2. Review the entire lesson. Be sure that you know how to make "Warm Fuzzies." If the class is made up of very young children, you may want to start a few for the children to finish.
3. Make copies of "For You to Take Home" page.

This Session in Brief

Getting Started (10 min)

Building Community

Developing the Session

Bible Study (20 min)
Brainstorming (10 min)
Warm Fuzzies (10 min)

Concluding the Session (10 min)

Closing

The Session Plan

Getting Started

Building Community

Remind the children that this will be the last session but that the leaders will still be available to answer any questions the children have or provide any help they might need.

Developing the Session

Bible Study

Tell the children about Romans 8:35–39 and have them read along with the scripture printed on the "For You to Take Home" page. Explain the vocabulary in the passage ("conquerors," "spirit beings," etc.). (See "Theological and Biblical Concepts" for help with this important information.) Discuss the passage.

- Paul makes a list of things that cannot separate us from God. What are they?
- What are some things that we worry might separate us from God?
- Is there anything that keeps God's love from us?
- Can you think of a time when you worried that your family or a friend might not love you anymore?
- Can you think of a time when you worried that God might not love you anymore?
- How do you think the people felt when they heard this message about God's love?

Brainstorming

Ask the children to name the major things they have learned in this series of sessions. On newsprint or chalkboard, list the major topics, which should include:

- I am a child of God.
- My body belongs to me.
- My feelings are part of God's creation.
- My feelings are clues about what is happening to me.
- I can say "No!"
- God will comfort me.
- No one has the right to touch me and make me feel bad.
- God cares about suffering of people.
- I have learned ways to protect myself.
- God gives me strength.
- I can talk to a trusted adult.
- The church can be a place to go for help.
- People who have hurt someone should be sorry for what they have done.
- God loves me.

NOTE TO THE TEACHER

This activity is meant to encourage the children to respond to the whole course of sessions. This review should also be personal. Encourage the children to use their own words to name these topics. Add any topics that the children miss. This activity is also an excellent way to evaluate the sessions. The teachers should be able to tell which topics the children remember and which had the greatest impact on the children.

Warm Fuzzies

Tell the children about warm fuzzies.

A Warm Fuzzy is a soft ball of yarn. When a person has a Warm Fuzzy, he or she has warm, happy, and loving feelings. A Warm Fuzzy can also be kind words, a good hug, or just the experience of being with a good friend or someone who cares about us.

The Warm Fuzzy made of yarn reminds us of the experiences that we have had when we feel good about ourselves. It also reminds us of times when our friends and family have helped us feel good about ourselves. A Warm Fuzzy is also a good reminder of God's love. No matter what situation we find ourselves in, we can remember God's love. God's love can help us feel better.

Explain how to make a Warm Fuzzy. Choose a color of yarn; children can choose their favorite color. Wrap the yarn around the around the 2-inch side of the cardboard rectangle until a fat bundle is made. Then slide the yarn off the cardboard and tie the center tightly with a string that is stronger than yarn. Then cut the loops. Finally, fluff up your Warm Fuzzy.

NOTE TO THE TEACHER

Warm Fuzzies can be used in a variety of settings to help children focus on the positive experience of being loved and cared for. For a child who has experienced abuse, the Warm Fuzzy can be a symbol of hope. For all children, the Warm Fuzzy can be a reminder of God's love. Although younger children can best understand concrete, physical things, they can also understand that something physical, like a Warm Fuzzy, can remind us of something that can't be seen. Giving each child a Warm Fuzzy allows them to take home something physical that will remind them of God's love in the future.

Concluding the Session

Closing

Ask the children to bring their Warm Fuzzies with them as they sit in a circle.

Ask the children to name one positive thing they learned during this class. Give each child a few minutes.

Remind the group that the teachers are available even after the course is over. Suggest ways that they might contact a teacher.

Sing together any of the songs learned during this course. In closing, read together the scripture from Romans 8 found on the "For You to Take Home" page.

For You to Take Home

In today's session we learned:

• God loves each child.

Here's the scripture for today's lesson.

Who would put us apart from the love of Christ?
Can hunger, sickness, floods, wars, poverty, mistreatment,
*   or abuse?*
No!
In all these things we are more than conquerors through
*   the one who loved us.*
We are sure that neither death nor life,
*   Nor spirit beings, nor nations*
*   Nor things present, nor things to come,*
*   Nor powers, nor height, nor depth,*
*   Nor anything else in all creation,*
Will be able to put us apart from the love of God in Christ Jesus.
[Romans 8:35-39, Native American Translation]

Appendix A
Sexual Abuse Fact Sheet[1]

- Child sexual abuse is defined as sexual contact with a child through force or trickery. This includes obscene phone calls, fondling, intercourse, anal or oral sex, prostitution, and pornography.
- Incestuous parents may love their children but put their sexual/intimacy needs before the needs of their children. Sometimes this is because of a crisis period in their lives or because boundaries in the family are confused or unclear.
- The average victim of child sexual abuse is between eight and eleven years old.
- Some experts estimate that five or six children in a typical classroom of thirty have been affected by sexual abuse, regardless of geographic area, race, or socioeconomic class.
- Men are responsible for 90 to 97 percent of abuse cases, at least in cases currently reported.
- Between 60 and 90 percent of victims of child sexual abuse are girls.
- Offenders are not usually strangers to children—70 to 80 percent of offenders are known to children.
- Half of the child victims are molested in their own home or in the offender's home.
- Heterosexual males present greater risk to boys and girls than homosexual males.
- The average length of an incestuous relationship is three years; it is rarely a one-time occurrence.
- The victim may cope in many ways: by being withdrawn, delinquent, or an over-achiever in school. Victims of sexual abuse are typically not as involved with their peers as other children.

Appendix B
Indicators of Sexual Abuse
in Children[1]

The following physical and behavioral characteristics may signal that a child is a victim of sexual abuse. As with other lists of symptoms, some of the same signs may indicate other types of problems. Until recently, sexual abuse was not often considered as a possible reason for erratic or problem behavior. It is important to recognize that sexual abuse is a possibility when a child/adolescent exhibits several of the following behaviors.

Physical Signs

Bruising, bleeding, or infections in the genital/anal area. Physical symptoms may be manifested as difficulty in walking, sitting, or urinating; scratching or tugging at clothing around the genital area; torn, stained, or bloody clothing; genito-urinary complaints or infections.

It is also possible that there are no physical indicators that a child is being abused.

Behavioral/Attitudinal Signs

- Eating, sleeping, or eliminating disturbances
- Recurrent physical complaints
- Withdrawn or aggressive behavior
- Tired, lethargic, sleepy appearance
- Fear or suspicion of adults
- Sexually explicit language or behavior not appropriate to the child's age
- Regressive behavior such as whining, excessive crying, thumbsucking, wetting, or soiling self
- Aversion to a particular person, place, or situation
- Change in school performance, truancy
- Fear, worry, over-seriousness, depression
- Anger toward or dislike of adults, authority figures
- Running away from home
- Suicide threats or attempts
- Behavioral defiance, sexual promiscuity, prostitution
- Shy, withdrawn, overburdened appearance
- Substance abuse that is more than experimental
- Reluctance to undress for physical education
- Stealing, shoplifting
- Pregnancy wishes
- Interest in early marriage

- Attraction to older men or dislike of men
- Excessive hand washing, bathing
- Unreasonably restricted social activities or overly protective father
- Poor self-image, low self-esteem
- Fantasies about victimization or violence
- Alienation from family members, rejection of typical family affection
- Fear of strange men and/or strange situations
- Overly clinging or dependent behavior
- Extreme avoidance of touch
- Abrupt change in behavior or personality
- Extreme overachieving

Appendix C

How to Help a Child Victim of Sexual Abuse

Anytime during the teaching of this unit, a group member may disclose that he or she either has experienced or is currently experiencing sexual abuse. The first reactions of an adult to whom a child talks are very important.

Many adults' first instinct is to ask questions to find out whether the experience is true or untrue. It is essential that this task be left to the professionals.

Here are helpful suggestions for responding to a victim's disclosure:

1. Listen carefully to the child's account of his or her experience. This is a time to be loving and supportive.
2. Tell the child that you believe that he or she is telling you the truth. Reassure the child that what has happened is not his or her fault.
3. Thank the child for sharing with you and make it clear that you are very sorry that this has happened to him or her.
4. Explain that you will do everything you can to make the abuse stop. In order to help the child, you must tell other people who can help.

Above all, make it clear that you will stand with the child and that you will do everything you can to be supportive.

Appendix D
Reporting Child Sexual Abuse[1]

Teachers are often confused about what circumstances and with what procedures sexual abuse should be reported. Even when we feel confused, the question is not *should* we report (legally and morally we are required to) but rather *how* to report. Find out about your church policy, which may include guidelines stating to whom and how the formal report should be made.

When to Report

In all states, teachers, parents, administrators, nurses, social workers, and concerned citizens must legally report any suspicion of child sexual abuse. Fortunately, we do not required to investigate the reality of that suspicion. The Protective Services division of the state's Department of Public Welfare is legally mandated to do such an investigation. We should also keep in mind that, according to federal legislation (Public Act 93–247, January 31, 1974), each state must "have in effect a state child abuse and neglect law which includes provision for immunity for persons reporting . . . from prosecution" and that the report will be kept confidential.

Guidelines for Reporting

1. Whenever children tell you that they have had sexual contact with an adult (person over eighteen years old) involving (A) intercourse, (B) fondling or touching, (C) anal or oral sex, or (D) photographed, filmed, or videotaped in a sexual manner.
2. Whenever children tell you they have been forced or tricked into sexual conduct with another child (particularly a child five or more years older or a child sixteen to eighteen years old).
3. Whenever friends or acquaintances of a suspected victim report to you that the child has reported such abuse to them.
4. When physical evidence of sexual abuse is discovered (physical harm, irritation in genital areas, or venereal disease).

Be aware of the following indications that sexual abuse is or may have been going on:
1. Sudden change in mood or personality
2. Sudden change in school performance
3. Extreme withdrawal from social contacts with peers
4. Acting out behaviors—fighting, exhibitionism, drug usage, runaways
5. Seductive behaviors—learned from being used sexually
6. Aversion to touch or closeness; listlessness
7. Psychosomatic illnesses
8. Unusually high degree of fear and distrust of adults
9. Over-compliance in attempts to please adults
10. Lying or stealing

How to Report

If you have questions about reporting or need additional information, contact your Child Protective Services Unit, Department of Public Welfare. Report situations as soon as possible to facilitate services to children and families. Report even if the child states the abuse has ended or that they have already told someone about it. Protective Services' trained staff will do the investigation.

Your local Child Protective Service number is:

Appendix E

What Happens When a Report Is Made[1]

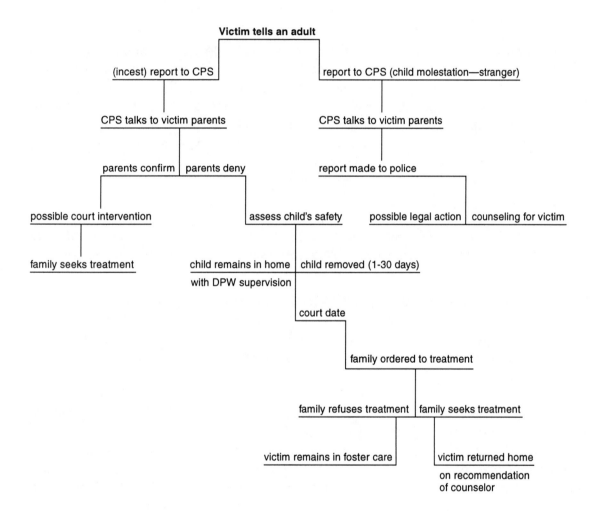

Victim tells an adult

(incest) report to CPS

report to CPS (child molestation—stranger)

CPS talks to victim parents

CPS talks to victim parents

parents confirm | parents deny

report made to police

possible court intervention

assess child's safety

possible legal action | counseling for victim

family seeks treatment

child remains in home | child removed (1-30 days)
with DPW supervision

court date

family ordered to treatment

family refuses treatment | family seeks treatment

victim remains in foster care

victim returned home
on recommendation
of counselor

Appendix F

Reporting Child Abuse: An Ethical Mandate for Ministry

Marie M. Fortune

The epidemic problem of child abuse in the United States (physical, sexual, and emotional) presents persons in ministry with a challenge and an opportunity. When child abuse is disclosed, the religious leader can intervene with sensitivity and compassion to bring an end to this suffering, which has most likely been chronic. Yet intervention by a minister is not necessarily forthcoming because of hesitancy, confusion, lack of information, and ambivalence. Situations of child abuse are complex, and a minister may well try a private solution and avoid using other community resources, usually to the detriment of the child and the family.

An Ethical Mandate

The ethical mandate for Christian ministry in response to the abused child is rooted in Jesus' gospel teachings. In Matthew, Jesus points to the child as the one who is the greatest in the realm:

> *Whoever welcomes one such child in my name welcomes me. If any of*
> *you put a stumbling block before one of these little ones who believe in*
> *me, it would be better for you if a great millstone were fastened around*
> *your neck and you were drowned in the depth of the sea.*
> *[Matthew 18:5–6]*

Jesus is consistent in his assertion of the specialness and value of children in a cultural context that regarded children as property of their father. He also points clearly to the responsibility of those around children to care for them. This teaching must have been consistent with Jesus' understanding of the Hebrew custom of hospitality, in which the orphan, widow, and sojourner were identified as being the responsibility of the entire community, which was to provide for their needs and protect them. What is at stake here is these persons' vulnerability, which is a consequence of their life circumstance. Children are by definition vulnerable and in a need of care and protection by adults. When this care and protection are not provided by adults, and when those whose responsibility it is to protect are in fact the source of pain and abuse for the child, then someone else must act to provide for the child. Such is the situation faced by a religious leader to whom it is disclosed that a child may be abused.

The other ethical principle that applies here is that of "justice-making" in response to harm done by one person to another. Christian scripture here is very specific: "Be on your guard! If another disciple sins, you must rebuke the offender, and if there is repentance, you must forgive" (Luke 17:3). The one who harms another must be confronted so that he might seek repentance. Both Hebrew and Christian scriptures are clear that repentance has to do with change: "Get yourselves a new heart and a new spirit! . . .

Turn, then, and live" (Ezekiel 18:31–32). The Greek word used for repentance is *metanoia*, "to have another mind." In this context of repentance, accountability, and justice, forgiveness and reconciliation may be possible. These should be primary concerns of the religious leader.

Final Goals

As with all forms of family violence, child abuse requires an immediate response and a recognition of a larger context. The goals of any effective response should follow this order:

1. Protect the child from further abuse.
2. Stop the abuser's violence.
3. Heal the victim's brokenness and, if possible, restore the family relationships; if not possible, mourn the loss of that relationship.

Taking these steps in order provides the best possible opportunity for eventual restoration of the family. Until the first two goals are successfully accomplished, the third is unachievable. It is certainly possible to have the victim and offender living in the same place and giving the appearance of being an intact family, but unless the victim is safe and the offender has taken steps to stop the abuse, there is no restoration and no intact family.

In situations of child abuse, these goals can best be accomplished by the early reporting of suspected child abuse to legal authorities. Every state in the United States provides a mechanism at the state level for reporting, investigating, assessing situations where children may be at risk. They also have the professional resources with which to assist victims, abusers, and other family members in addressing the three goals of intervention.

Reporting: Reasons to Report

1. *Facts about child abuse:*

Offenders will reoffend unless they get specialized treatment.
Offenders against children minimize, lie, and deny their abusive behavior.
Offenders rarely follow through on their good intentions or genuine remorse without help from the outside.
Treatment of offenders is most effective when it is ordered and monitored by the courts.
The pattern of the abuse must be broken in order to get help to the victim and offender.
Quick forgiveness of the offender is likely to be "cheap grace" and is unlikely to lead to repentance and change. These factors emphasize the need to use an external, authoritative, specialized resource in order to bring change for the family.

2. *Access to specialized resources for treatment:* Unless the ministers are specially trained to provide treatment for victims and abusers of family violence, they alone are not an adequate resource to the family. The pastor's role is critical throughout, but the most important first step is reporting.

3. *Access to a means to protect a child and require accountability from an offender:* The child protective service or law enforcement offices in a community are the only bodies authorized to investigate allegations of abuse, provide physical protection for a child, and restrain the behavior of an adult who is abusive.

4. *Deprivatizing the situation:* Involving the services of a community agency requires that the silence that has supported this chronic situation be broken. It is not simply a private, family matter; it is a community concern. The consequences can no longer be avoided. Again, this offers the best chance to provide help to a hurting family.

5. *Setting a norm:* Involvement of the wider community clearly communicates to all involved that the physical, sexual, or emotional abuse or neglect of a child is intolerable because children are important and it is our collective responsibility to protect them.

6. *Mandatory:* In every state, persons in helping professions are mandated to report the suspicion of child abuse to the authorities. In some states, the religious leader is exempt from this requirement. In every state, any citizen *may* report suspected child abuse and not be liable for an unfounded report if the report is made in good faith. With or without a legal mandate, clergy should consider the weight of an ethical mandate to report.

Why Ministers May Hesitate

The ambivalence many ministers feel about reporting child abuse comes at the point when other considerations supersede the fundamental goal of protecting the child. Such things as protecting family privacy or the status of the adults in the family, fears of breaking up the family, or perceptions of the social service providers as punitive or insensitive to the religious beliefs of the family make it difficult for a religious leader to refer or report. Yet once ministers receive a disclosure, they have the authority and responsibility to protect children who cannot protect themselves.

Reporting: How-To's

Sometimes the hesitancy to report comes from a lack of understanding of what will happen once a report is made. Every state has a statewide agency responsible for child protection.[1] Generally, a report is made to indicate there is suspicion that a child is being harmed. The religious leader need not have specific evidence and need not attempt to gather evidence or detailed information from the person who discloses. If it sounds as if abuse may have occurred and the child is still at risk, then the child protection agency should be notified. It will investigate the situation and assess the risk to the child. In some communities, it will encourage the alleged abuser to temporarily leave the home. Frequently, when there is no other available option, it will remove the child temporarily from the home. If there is evidence of abuse, it will take the case to the prosecutor, who will then decide whether to file charges. Whether charges are filed or not, the child protection agency will offer counseling to the child victim and nonoffending family members. If the abuser is convicted, the court may mandate counseling as an alternative to prison time. Adults seldom serve time for child abuse convictions.

Problems and Suggestions

Another cause for hesitation in the religious leader is the fear that reporting will be perceived by abusers as turning them in and thus will damage, perhaps irrevocably, the pastoral relationship. Two factors militate against this fear. First, it is seldom the abuser who discloses; it is most likely the child/teenage victim or the nonoffending family member who calls for help. Second, the way in which the report is made significantly shapes the perception of the person who has disclosed.

For example, if a religious leader conveys any ambivalence to someone at their first hint of abuse by saying, "Don't tell me any more or I will have to report this," the context is set for a punitive and secretive situation. The minister is also withholding possible assistance from the person who is seeking help. Further, it is not helpful for the minister to listen to a disclosure, never indicating that a report must be made, then wait until the person leaves to call and report anonymously. This may relieve the conscience, but does not help create a context in which the religious leader can continue to minister as part of wider intervention.

Instead, it is helpful when hearing a disclosure to indicate that additional help will be needed in order to aid the victim, save the family, help the abuser, and so forth, and that the best resource to begin with is the child protection service. Suggest that the person who has disclosed call the agency with you present, and offer to be with them when the social service provider comes to talk with them. Help the person disclosing to understand that the child protection worker can provide much more in addition to what you can do, and reassure the discloser that you will not desert him or her. Then seek to work with the child protective service worker to provide for the needs of the members of the family seeking help.

What to Expect with Disclosure/Reporting

Offenders will frequently be the last people you would expect to sexually molest a child. They may well be highly regarded, upstanding citizens who are active in the congregation. Do not allow your impression of these people in public settings to prevent you from entertaining the possibility that they may have molested a child.

Initially, the offender will usually deny all responsibility and will seek to discredit the victim's story by attacking its credibility: "She lies about everything, but this is the most ridiculous one she's told yet." It is always tempting to believe the adult's denial because our society has never taken children's words very seriously.

Very rarely do victims falsely report an offense. If they have summoned the courage to tell someone about their situation, they almost always have been harmed by someone. Victims may also quickly recant their story because they feel extreme pressure from family members and maybe even the offender to do so. Their recantation does not mean the abuse did not occur or that this person is now safe. Nonoffending family members (usually mothers) initially may not believe their child, but instead feel pressure to support the offender against the child. The mother may also be a victim of spouse abuse.

When a report is made to the legal authorities, chaos usually erupts. The whole family is in crisis. It may take several weeks for this very complex situation to be sorted out. The results of disclosure and reporting may not be a final resolution to the incestuous abuse situation in a family, but some attention to this matter is better than none.

Special Considerations

Confessions and Confidentiality

Many people in pastoral roles perceive a contradiction between their obligation to preserve confidentiality of communication with a congregant and their obligation to report the suspicion of child abuse. They see this contradiction as a conflict of ethical demands. Part of the perceived conflict arises from the interpretation of confidentiality and its purpose, particularly as it rests within the responsibility of the religious professional. The context for an analysis of these ethical demands is the understanding of confidentiality that comes to the religious professional from multiple sources.

The purpose of confidentiality has been to provide a safe place for a congregant or client to share concerns, questions, or burdens without fear of disclosure. It provides a context of respect and trust, within which help can hopefully be provided for an individual. It has meant that some people have come forward seeking help who might not otherwise have done so out of fear of punishment or embarrassment. Confidentiality has traditionally been the ethical responsibility of the professional within a professional relationship and is generally assumed to be operative even if a specific request has not been made by the congregant or client.

For the minister, unlike the secular helping professional, confidentiality rests in the context of spiritual issues and expectations. In Christian denominations, the expectations of confidentiality lie most specifically within the experience of confession. The responsibility of the pastor or priest ranges from a strict understanding to a more flexible one—from the letter to the spirit of the law. For example, for Anglican and Roman Catholic priests, the confessional occasion with a penitent person is sacramental; whatever information is revealed is held in confidence by the seal of confession, with no exceptions.[2] The United Methodist *Book of Discipline* does not view confession as sacramental but states, "Ministers . . . are charged to maintain all confidences inviolate, including confessional confidences."[3] The Lutheran Church in America protects the confidence of the parishioner and allows for the discretion of the pastor: "no minister . . . shall divulge any confidential disclosure given to him in the course of his care of souls or otherwise in his professional capacity, except with the express permission of the person who has confided in him or in order to prevent a crime."[4] Even within Christian denominations, there is a range of interpretations of the expectations of confidentiality that are not necessarily limited to the confessional occasion.

What Are Confidentiality and Secrecy?

It may be useful in this discussion to make a distinction between confidentiality and secrecy. Secrecy is the absolute promise never under any circumstance to share any information that comes to a member of the clergy; this is the essence of sacramental confession. But a commitment to secrecy may also support maintaining the secret of child abuse, which likely means that the abuse will continue. Confidentiality means to hold information in trust and to share it with others only in the interest of the person involved, with their permission, in order to seek consultation with another professional. Information may also be shared without violating confidentiality in order to protect others from harm. Confidentiality is intended as a means to help an individual get help for a problem and prevent further harm to herself or others. Confidentiality is not intended to protect abusers from being held accountable for their actions or to keep them from getting the help they need. Shielding them from the consequence of their behavior will likely further endanger their victims and will deny them the repentance they need.

In addition, confidentiality is not intended to protect professionals; it is for those whom they serve. It should not be used as a shield to protect incompetent or negligent colleagues, or to protect them from professional obligations. Thus, confidentiality may be invoked for all the wrong reasons and not truly in the interest of a particular congregant or of society. This was never the intent of this special provision of pastoral communication.

Disclosure Within Different Faiths

When a disclosure is made by an offender in a confessional setting, the religious leader has the opportunity to respond within the parameters of a particular faith's tradition while keeping in mind the overriding priority of protecting the child victim. For example, a Roman Catholic priest can hear the confession of a child abuser, prescribe penance to report himself to the child protection service, and withhold absolution until the penance is accomplished. Confession to a priest does not carry with it the priest's obligation to absolve in the absence of penitent acts. Confession opens the opportunity for the penitent persons to repent and to make right the harm they have done to others. Likewise, for a Protestant in a nonsacramental confessional situation, directives may be given and actions prescribed that include the abuser reporting himself to child protection services. If it is clear that the penitent will not follow the directive of the religious leader and self-report, then some Protestant ministers have the option and the obligation to report directly. The vulnerability of the child and the significant likelihood that the abuser will continue supersede an obligation to maintain in confidence the confession of the penitent.

Cooperation: Working with Secular Service Providers

In addition to a long-standing breach between religious and secular professionals concerned with mental health issues, some substantive concerns have often prevented ministers from working effectively with social service providers or therapists. All these concerns come to the fore when the issue of reporting child abuse is raised: separation of church and state, involvement of the criminal justice system, disregard for a family's religious beliefs, and breaking up families. While the state should not interfere with the practice of ministry, it does have the lawful responsibility of protecting children from harm. The church should see this as a common agenda and work with those designated to carry out this mandate. Even with its multitude of shortcomings (not the least of which are sexism and racism), the criminal justice system can provide a mechanism to enforce accountability for offenders and should not be avoided to protect offenders from embarrassment or the serious consequences of their abuse. A family's religious beliefs deserve respect. But any effort by family members to use religious beliefs to justify abuse of a child or deflect intervention intended to stop abuse should be challenged by both religious and secular professionals. Finally, outside intervention to protect a child does not break up the family. The abuse that preceded the intervention broke up the family and endangered its members. Temporary separation of family members may well be the only possible means of healing and restoration, and should be used when appropriate.

Cooperation between religious and secular professionals expands the resources available to a family experiencing abuse. The special skills each can bring are much need by family members. Religious leaders can concentrate on their pastoral responsibilities in concert with the social service provider, who can guide the intervention and treatment.

Conclusion

Situations of suspected child abuse are seldom simple and straightforward. Religious leaders should be guided by a commitment to the overriding priority of protection of children and by a clear sense of the limits of their own resources. The mechanism of reporting child abuse and the resources that follow from it are invaluable tools for the minister. Clarity of purpose will direct an ethical mandate to use every available means to stop the abuse of a child.

Notes

Introduction

1. Diana E. H. Russell, *Rape in Marriage* (New York: Macmillan, 1983).

2. David Finkelhor, *Child Sexual Abuse: New Theory and Research* (New York: Free Press, 1984).

3. Jennifer James, Principal Investigator, "Entrance into Juvenile Prostitution," August 1980; and "Entrance into Juvenile Male Prostitution," August 1982.

4. Juvenile Sex Offender Program, University of Washington, Seattle, Washington.

5. Marie Fortune, *Sexual Abuse Prevention: A Study for Teenagers* (New York: United Church Press, 1984), 9.

6. W. Jerome Berryman, *Godly Play* (New York: Harper, 1991).

Session 4

1. Adapted from Carol A. Plummer, *Preventing Sexual Abuse: Activities and Strategies for Those Working with Children and Adolescents* (Holmes Beach, Fla.: Learning Publications, 1984), 73.

Session 6

1. Fortune, *Sexual Abuse Prevention,* 22.

2. Adapted from Kathy Beland, *Talking About Touching* (Seattle: Committee for Children, 1988).

3. Adapted from Angela R. Carl, *Good Hugs and Bad Hugs* (Cincinnati: Standard Publishing, 1985).

Session 7

1. Carol A. Plummer, *Preventing Sexual Abuse: Activities and Strategies for Those Working with Children and Adolescents.* (Holmes Beach, Fla.: Learning Publications, 1984), 65. Used by permission.

Session 8

1. Adapted from Plummer, *Preventing Sexual Abuse*, 71. Used by permission.

Appendix A

1. Plummer, *Preventing Sexual Abuse*, 145. Used by permission.

Appendix B

1. Mary Nelson and Kay Clark, eds., *The Educator's Guide to Preventing Child Sexual Abuse* (Santa Cruz, Calif.: ETR, 1986), 182. Reprinted by permission of ETR Associates. For information about this and other related materials, call 1-800-321-4407.

Appendix D

1. Adapted from Plummer, *Preventing Sexual Abuse,* 157–58. Used by permission.

Appendix E

1. Plummer, *Preventing Sexual Abuse*, 159. Used by permission.

Appendix F

1. Religious leaders should familiarize themselves with the child protective services office in their community. Some child protection programs only investigate possible abuse; others both investigate and provide treatment. Ask about the specifics of the agency's approach to reports and the options available to them. Approach them as a professional ally and resource. Invite them to a discussion with local ministerial groups.

2. See Seward Reese, 1963, "Confidential Communications to Clergy," *Ohio State Law Journal,* 24:55.

3. *The Book of Discipline of the United Methodist Church*, 1980 (Nashville, Tenn.: United Methodist Publishing House, 1980), 220, paragraph 440.4.

4. The Minutes of the United Lutheran Church in America, 22nd Biennial Convention, 1960, as quoted in Reese, op. cit., 69.

Appendix G

1. *Everyone's United Nations*, 9th ed. (New York: United Nations, 1979), 412–23.

Resources on Sexual Violence

Child Sexual Abuse—A Handbook for Clergy and Church Members, by Lee W. Carlson. Valley Forge, Pa.: Judson Press, 1988.

> *A practical and accessible resource for clergy and lay leaders.*

The Child Sexual Abuse Prevention Guidebook, by Cordelia Kent. Sexual Assault Services, Hennepin County Attorney's Office, Minneapolis, Minnesota 19079.

> *The concept of "touch continuum" has been further developed through physical (dance and theater) interaction with many groups of children along with materials for teaching by Ms. Kent.*

Feeling Safe, Feeling Strong: How to Avoid Sexual Abuse and What to Do If It Happens to You, by Susan N. Terkel and Janice E. Rench. Minneapolis: Lerner Publications, 1984.

> *Written for children between the ages of 8 and 12, this book can be read by a child alone or with a trusted adult. It includes seven stories that describe situations of children in sexual abuse. The specific topics are: personal rights, pornography, exhibitionism, incest, obscene phone calls, and rape. The book emphasizes problem-solving.*

Good Hugs and Bad Hugs: How Can You Tell?, by Angela R. Carl. Cincinnati: Standard Publishing, 1985.

> *This activity book is intended for use with the parent/teacher book Child Abuse! What You Can Do About It to train children in sexual abuse prevention. Children, kindergarten through sixth grade, will learn how to identify potentially dangerous situations, how to avoid abuse, how to deal with it if it happens, and how to seek help from a trusted adult.*

He Told Me Not to Tell, by Jennifer Fay. King County Rape Relief, Seattle, Wash. 91979.

> *This book is a guide for talking to children about sexual assault. Information encourages parents to use correct body-part names, back up their children when they say "no," and identify assault victims.*

No More Secrets for Me, by Oralee Wachter. Boston and Toronto: Little, Brown, 1982.

> *A book for children to read alone or with a trusted adult, it tells about four different children whose rights have been abused and what they did in their situations.*

Preventing Child Sexual Abuse: A Curriculum for Children Ages 9–12, by Kathryn Goering Reid with Marie M. Fortune. New York: Pilgrim Press, 1989.

> *This religious education curriculum is designed for church school, vacation Bible school, or other special educational events. It draws on excellent secular materials in the field and uses biblical materials as resources. This material also confronts misinterpretations of biblical materials that have been used to support abusive relationships.*

Preventing Sexual Abuse: Activities and Strategies for Those Working with Children and Adolescents, by Carol A. Plummer. Holmes Beach, Fla.; Learning Publications, 1984.

> *This curriculum is written for school teachers and counselors and contains a skeleton outline of a program for teaching prevention techniques. It also includes games and activities.*

Private Zone, by Frances S. Dayee. New York: Warner Community Co., 1982.

> *Written for children ages 3 to 9, the book focuses on "private zones" and who should touch a child. It explains that children have the right to say "no" and to tell another adult when inappropriate touching occurs.*

Sexual Abuse Prevention Education: An Annotated Bibliography, compiled by Key Clark. Santa Cruz, Calif.: Network Publications, 1985.

> *This inclusive bibliography details most books and films for adults, children, and youth in the area of sexual abuse prevention and lists film distributors. It is an essential listing for educators.*

Sexual Violence: The Unmentionable Sin, by Marie M. Fortune. New York: Pilgrim Press, 1983.

> *In this groundbreaking book, the author leads the reader through a carefully spelled out argument, first defining her subject matter— explaining how even the words "sexual violence" have been explained away from the perspective of the offender—and concluding with a thesis that can hardly be disputed: sexual violence undermines all levels of social well-being, and must be stopped. She also explores how the confusion arises between sexuality and sexual violence, explaining the difficult nature of consent.*

Talking About Touching for Parents and Kids—Parents Guide, by Kathy Beland. Seattle: Committee for Children, 1988.

> *This book has good information on teaching children about appropriate touching.*